BILLY'S
DICTIONARY
FOR BLOKES

Billy Brownless is a football legend. He retired in 1996 having played 198 games for the Geelong Football Club, including four losing grand finals. He likes to remind people that he once kicked a footy 80 metres over a silo, and booted the winning goal after the siren in the 1994 qualifying final. Billy is a regular on Channel Nine's *The Footy Show* and *Sunday Footy Show*, and co-host of Triple M's 'Rush Hour' drive-time program. He lives in Geelong with his wife, Nicky, and their four kids.

Billy Brownless

BILLY'S

DICKTIONARY
FOR BLOKES

An **A-Z** of essential words for the modern man

PENGUIN
MICHAEL
JOSEPH

MICHAEL JOSEPH

Published by the Penguin Group
Penguin Group (Australia)
250 Camberwell Road, Camberwell, Victoria 3124, Australia
(a division of Pearson Australia Group Pty Ltd)
Penguin Group (USA) Inc.
375 Hudson Street, New York, New York 10014, USA
Penguin Group (Canada)
90 Eglinton Avenue East, Suite 700, Toronto, Canada ON M4P 2Y3
(a division of Pearson Penguin Canada Inc.)
Penguin Books Ltd
80 Strand, London WC2R 0RL England
Penguin Ireland
25 St Stephen's Green, Dublin 2, Ireland
(a division of Penguin Books Ltd)
Penguin Books India Pvt Ltd
11 Community Centre, Panchsheel Park, New Delhi – 110 017, India
Penguin Group (NZ)
67 Apollo Drive, Rosedale, North Shore 0632, New Zealand
(a division of Pearson New Zealand Ltd)
Penguin Books (South Africa) (Pty) Ltd
24 Sturdee Avenue, Rosebank, Johannesburg 2196, South Africa

Penguin Books Ltd, Registered Offices: 80 Strand, London WC2R 0RL, England

First published by Penguin Group (Australia), 2011

10 9 8 7 6 5 4 3 2 1

Cover and text design by Nikki Townsend © Penguin Group (Australia)
Cover photographs and chapter openers by James Penlidis
Typeset in PMN Caecilia by Post Pre-press Group, Brisbane, Queensland
Printed and bound in Australia by McPherson's Printing Group, Maryborough, Victoria

National Library of Australia
Cataloguing-in-Publication data:

Brownless, Anthony William, 1967–
Billy's dictionary for blokes : an A to Z of essential words for the modern man /
Billy Brownless.
9781921518805 (pbk.)
Men – Australia – Social life and customs – Dictionaries.
Wit and humor – Dictionaries.
Australia – Social life and customs – Dictionaries.

305.3103

penguin.com.au

DEDICATION

To my dear mum, who passed away
while I was writing this book.
I got all my brains and literary talent
from her – thanks, Mum.

INTRODUCTION

I went looking for a dictionary on the family bookshelf the other day. I'll be honest, it's been a while since I picked one up. The last one I remember seeing had 'Bill Brownless, Year 10 Assumption College' written on the inside cover. I flogged it to another kid at the school: 'Dictionary for sale – hardly used. As good as new'.

In fact, most of my textbooks were pretty much kept in mint condition. I lost my locker key in the first week of school and didn't do anything about it for that whole year. Those books were still looking pristine when the maintenance guys used boltcutters to break into my locker on the last day of school. It wasn't all good, though. I forgot I'd locked my lunch in there as well. I've smelled some bad stuff in my time but that is easily the worst thing to have ever made its way up my nostrils. Three kids who were there at the time spent the rest of the day in the sick bay.

The school cleaned out my locker, sprayed it and the whole room with industrial-strength deodoriser, but to this day they have never been rid of the smell completely. I just hope that my excellently kept textbooks were of some use to the kids who inherited them. I'm glad I passed them on. I feel as if I've donated my organs to give someone else a better quality of life. It's actually good that I gave books because my organs are pretty much stuffed. In fact, if any of those people who received one my books would like to repay me by donating a liver, that'd be great.

Why was I looking for a dictionary, you might ask. I was playing Scrabble. I know what you're thinking: Billy playing

Scrabble? He wouldn't even know what the box looks like. What happened was that my mate brought it around because he's always trying to find a game that he can beat me at. He obviously thought: Scrabble, that involves words, and words mightn't be Billy's strong point. Sure, I'm probably not what you'd call a master of the English language, but I do talk a lot. A real lot. That involves using words, doesn't it? In a day, I'd use heaps of words. It'd be hundreds of words – no, probably thousands. Sure, most of the time it'd be the same word, especially if I'm having a bad day on the punt or the Cats are getting a rough deal from the umps.

One thing I learned playing Scrabble is that there are two types of dictionaries: big boring ones and pocket-sized boring ones and neither one has a definition for the word 'Cocko'. Turns out, many of the words I use aren't in your everyday dictionary or, worse, may not even exist. My solution? Bring out my own dictionary. I've always been a very practical (I hope I spelt that right) man, and what better way is there to justify using some of the words I do? Now I can just pull my dictionary off the shelf and say, 'It is a word! It says so right here!'

It would've been really handy in that game of Scrabble. I could've got 'Cocko' across the line. Before my mate had a chance to open his big mouth and question it, I would've come straight back with, 'According to this dictionary "Cocko" means friend or mate. "Often used to refer to any male you are greeting." In fact, not just males. When the lady at the fish-and-chip shop gives me my order, I always say, "Thanks, Cocko!" ' That would've sat him on his backside quick smart and given him something to think about. More importantly, it would've scored me 13 points. On a triple-word score that would've added up to three times 13, which is . . . um . . . hang on . . . give me a minute . . . 39. Yep, 39. If I'd ever taken my maths book out of my locker, I may have been able to work that one out a bit quicker.

So, here it is! A reference book of words for me and any other blokes out there. I have a sneaking suspicion there could be quite a few of you. No longer will we be made fun of by those who reckon we just make stuff up or have no idea what we're talking about. If these words are being used by all of us, every day of the week, then they must exist and need to be recognised officially. Hopefully this book will be very useful in a variety of situations: at home, at work, at a barbecue with friends, on the bus, on the train, at the supermarket, at the footy and especially during a game of Scrabble. Here's an idea – punch a hole in it and attach it to your key ring. Then you can take it with you everywhere you go. Or even better, put wheels on it and hook it onto the back of your car. Wow! The first ever trailer/dictionary. It doesn't get any more blokey than that. You're a genius, Billy!

I've also included words that we should know the meaning of because they somehow relate to our lives.

❁ These are 'Chick words', words that our wives, partners and girlfriends use. (In order to stay one step ahead of the enemy, you need to be able to break their code.)

★ ·TEENAGE SPEAK· These are definitions for some of the words (or lack thereof) that our kids use. We need to know what they are talking about because it often involves costing us money. At the rate at which young people are reducing whole sentences to a couple of letters or a smiley face, our language as we know it will probably die out by the year 2020. This book may be all we have left by then.

Billy

3

'A' isn't my favourite letter going around. It reminds me too much of what I was unable to achieve at school. I was more of your middle-of-the-road student. I only wish I'd been bad enough to get an 'F' because with a matching coloured pen and a bit of creative genius you could easily change an 'F' into an 'A'. That'd just leave me with the problem of convincing everyone I was capable of getting an 'A'. Hmm, no one would have bought that.

It's not only school marks that have the letter 'A' at the top of the tree. You have your 'A-list celebrities'. Yep, again, I come in at about a 'C'. Our national soccer league is called the 'A-League'. Again, let's be honest, sitting at around a 'C'. A lot of businesses use the 'A1' letter–number combination as part of their name because it makes them sound good. 'A1 Blinds and Drapes' or 'A1 Concrete'. Let's face it, who's gonna take their car to be fixed at 'B2 Motors'? Anyway, here are some words starting with 'A' that I reckon all blokes need to know.

a over t: arse over tit.

If you have a really bad fall, usually one that makes other people laugh, you're considered to have gone 'a over t'. With my man boobs, it is always a very appropriate description.

Ablett: legends. Snr and Jnr.

A bit of shine has come off Jnr since he did a runner. He won't have the privilege of finishing his career with the mighty Cats. That's one of two privileges Snr has up on him. The other one, of course, being that Snr got to play alongside one of the greats of the game – me.

AC/DC: bisexual.

Also a great band. Still rocking out at their age – unbelievable. Sold out at a heap of venues around the country for a series of concerts in 2010. That's the band, not the bisexuals.

ages: a really long time.

More than a couple of days, I reckon. Could be longer. Come to think of it, when I was a kid, our cat went missing for ages, and that was about two years. After that he waltzed back in as if nothing had happened, not even taking into account how upset we'd been that he'd walked out on us two years earlier.

aggro: really angry. Pissed off.

Lots of beers can sometimes increase the aggro. So, what you need to do is have even more beers to help you get past the aggro and into Noddyland.

air guitar: playing an imaginary guitar to music.

Most blokes start doing this at a young age and are masters at it by the time they become adults. Our cricketers and tennis players may be letting us down at an international level but our air guitarists are always winning heaps of competitions all over the world.

amber fluid: beer.

Often used when describing a big night. 'Had a bit too much of the old amber fluid.' I haven't used the expression for ages. It's a lot quicker and easier just to say 'VB'. I'm afraid 'amber fluid' isn't as popular as it used to be, and is being phased out by us blokes. We may need to put it on the endangered-bloke-speak list.

American: loud-mouthed tourist.

Would make good crocodile food. Don't get me wrong, I like a lot of Americans but there has to be something not quite right about a population that once thought George Bush was the best person to represent them. On the positive side, Oprah's audience was pretty friendly when she brought them with her to Australia. I thought Oprah gave it a good shake when she announced the trip on her show: 'We're going to AU . . . STRA . . . LI . . . AAAAAA!!!!' There's one Australian woman in the audience going, 'Great, just great. I've already paid for my bloody ticket home.'

amethyst: a purple stone used in jewellery.

Chicks mention it now and then, and now you know what it is. Take note – it's not the most expensive of stones.

Angelina: Jolie. Hot, very hot.

Don't let anyone tell you different. I've heard rumblings, mainly from chicks, that Angelina is losing her hotness. Don't fall for it; she's still got it. Brad Pitt isn't hanging around for a haircut.

Angus Young: see AC/DC.
The bit about the band not the bisexuals.

anklebiters: kids.
I had a nephew who used to really bite my ankles. His parents weren't much help either. Every time the kid got upset, they'd just tell him to go and chew on Uncle Billy's ankles for a while. There's still a patch on both my ankles where hair doesn't grow.

anniversary: whatever you do, don't forget it!
If it's the night before and you've forgotten it, go to one of those all-night florists, buy out the whole shop and then make an offer for whatever jewellery the attendant is wearing.

ANZAC: Australian and New Zealand Army Corps.
A lot of people get that wrong. It's important we all remember that, especially now that the ANZAC Day holiday is better known for being the day Collingwood and Essendon play a game of footy. It's great of those clubs to still let the diggers march on that day, I reckon.

apeshit, go: to lose control of your temper.
I don't think I've ever had a football coach who hasn't gone apeshit. Usually at me. Malcolm Blight used to go apeshit all the time. You could set your watch by it. Once I tried to calm him down by throwing him a banana. It didn't go down too well. I wonder if apes use the term 'apeshit' when one of them gets angry? Maybe they say, 'Hey, you should've seen Barry; he went elephantshit.'

aphrodisiac: something that improves your performance in the bedroom.

I always find that when the wife takes off her fluffy slippers it helps. She says that my switching off the footy helps. I'm not too sure about that: if the Cats get a good run on, I get fired up like there's no tomorrow. There are lots of different aphrodisiacs available, some natural and some man-made. You can buy those nasal sprays. Still, I'm not sure how spraying something up your nose can affect how things work way down there. Why wouldn't you just spray it down your undies? Historically, rhinoceros horn has been considered an aphrodisiac, which would give a rhino no excuse for being a dud in the sack. Imagine what it would've been like in the old days. Your missus wanted a bit of action, so off you went to tackle a rhino and cut off its horn. By the time you got home the moment would have passed. It's important to note that the whole rhino-horn-aphrodisiac thing hasn't been scientifically proven, which must be a massive relief for the rhinos.

apologise: to say sorry.

 A very useful thing for blokes to do. Apologising has got me out of much trouble, even when it wasn't my fault. Sometimes I'll walk into the house, notice that the Darl has a funny look on her face and apologise straightaway. Then I'll spend the next ten minutes trying to suss out exactly what I've apologised for. I think they just love hearing you say the word 'sorry'. If you add some flowers and chocolates in as well, you'll be sitting pretty for a good couple of weeks. Sorry for writing this bit, Darl. I really am.

app: application.

If you've got an Apple iPhone, you'll be very familiar with apps. There are heaps of them. My mate spent a lot of money on the iPhone 4, and the first app he got was this farting one. Every time you shake the phone it makes a fart sound. I couldn't believe it. He had a choice of hundreds of apps and that was the one he chose. I told him he was better than that, and he justified it by saying that it wasn't just the same fart sound every time. There are different ones. I told him to forget the iPhone – pull my finger and you'll get that app for free.

apples (she'll be): everything will be okay.

We try to make people feel at ease by telling them that 'she'll be apples'. Kevin Rudd was told by members of the Labor Party that 'she'll be apples' when he heard there was going to be a leadership challenge. Problem was, there were a few rotten apples in the ranks.

aromatherapy: this is that thing chicks do where they burn oils in the house which makes it smell good and supposedly provides some sort of therapeutic benefit.

Aromatherapy burner: a thing that holds candles and oils that smell. Just remember: there is nothing essential about this dust collector. Nothing. Try to throw it out or break it.

It's had the opposite effect on me. I'm always burning my bloody fingers whenever I move one of those candle holder thingos. It's always in the worst possible spot, like on the coffee table, so that I can't put my feet up, or on the bedroom dresser, where I usually throw my dirty clothes. I don't even know why they call them 'essential oils'. What's so essential about them? I hid them from my wife once. Four weeks went by and we were still breathing and stayed well and truly alive. Not so essential after all, are they?

arvo: afternoon.

For some reason it sounds best when it's said as 'Satdee arvo'. It's okay to spend an arvo lying on the couch because it's only an 'arvo'. It's a lazy-sounding sort of time. You haven't missed anything serious. The morning sounds far more important.

ASIO: Australian Security Intelligence Organisation.

It's Australia's spy agency. Like the CIA in America and MI5 in the UK. Ours just doesn't sound as exciting as those ones. Not sure what we need our own spies for anyway. It's not like we've got any master villains here who have built their evil headquarters in an old volcano. I heard Andrew Demetriou tried but he couldn't get the building permits for it. I think we're fairly safe in this country. Unless, of course, there was a threat to our beer supply, in which case our secret service agents should be called into action and given a licence to kill.

When your kids text you and you read 'ATM' it doesn't mean they want money. They're not talking about the old 'hole in the wall'. 'Busy ATM' means 'piss off, Dad, you're embarrassing me.'

ATM: automatic teller machine.

Some people might not know that's what the letters actually stand for because I'm forever being asked where the ATM machine is. In other words, they're really asking where the automatic teller machine machine is. When you go to the ATM, a message comes up on the screen telling you to use your hand to shield your PIN. If that is the best they've got to offer in terms of security, then we're all in a lot of trouble.

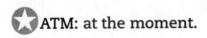 ATM: at the moment.

au naturel: in the natural state.

A lot of us blokes say it because it makes us sound educated. If it's our turn to cook dinner and we can't be stuffed doing the cooking part, we often present the uncooked food as 'au naturel'. Also used by us blokes when we are caught walking around the house in the nude. We're often very proud of ourselves no matter how out of shape our bodies are. Yeah, au naturel! I'm actually au naturel as I sit at the kitchen table writing this.

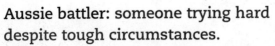

Aussie battler: someone trying hard despite tough circumstances.

We love a little Aussie battler. We like to barrack for them. Some of our most successful citizens started as Aussie battlers. Paul Hogan was a painter on the Sydney Harbour Bridge. His job was to maintain the youthful look of our great icon. He now spends his time trying to maintain the youthful look of his own face.

Aussie pizza: traditional fare found in most pizza shops.

Ingredients include mozzarella, ham, and an egg on top, and it's usually preceded by lots and lots of beers. I love all things Aussie but I just can't get my head around the Aussie pizza. Ham, egg and cheese – what's so Aussie about that? If it had a steak and some chips on it

with a piece of flake and a couple of dim sims, I might be interested.

ava: have a.
Yep, one of many examples of us turning two words into one. I'm a big fan of 'ava'. Ava nice day, ava good one, ava top night and ava great time reading my book.

avocado: a green pear-shaped fruit that chicks like to have on stuff.
They love it. It's got a massive pip. Avoid swallowing it. Blokes should never ask for it, especially in front of other blokes; it's embarrassing. It's used a lot in sushi (chick food). The Darl sent me down to buy an avocado once. I don't recommend it because it's hard to pick a ripe one. You have to softly squeeze them to get one that's just right. It feels weird doing it and you look pretty stupid too.

Avocado on toast:
An apology for breakfast. Watch out for this — as breakfast, it is not suitable for blokes.

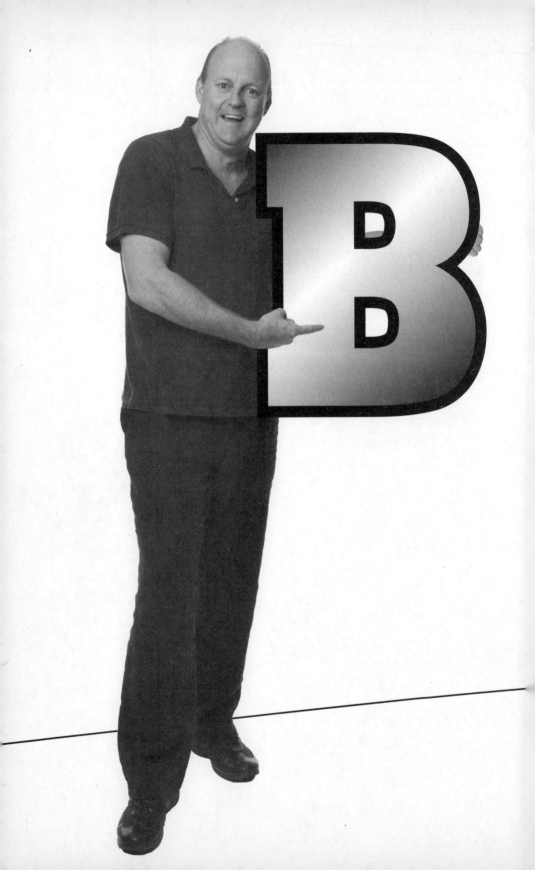

To B or not to B, that is the question, and that is probably the only thing from Shakespeare I know. Don't get me wrong, I don't have a problem with the bloke. He must've been a good writer if we're still talking about him. Besides, us authors need to stick together. I'm really attached to the letter 'B'. It's nice and round, like me. I use it a lot because I'm always writing my name some-where. Usually on cheques for things the Darl has bought or on Geelong memorabilia that a Cats' fan doesn't realise will be worth a lot less by having my name on it. Sure, 'Billy' is one of the most important words starting with B that blokes need to know, but here are a few more that may come in handy.

backtrack: what blokes do when the missus has caught us doing something wrong.

Whether you come home late or drunk or come home late *and* drunk, you always cop a barrage of abuse that sees you fumbling for words and saying stuff just to save your own arse. Sometimes it's easier not to come home at all, but don't wait too long or you'll get home to find that locks have been changed.

backwash: the stuff that goes out of your mouth and back into the orange juice after you drink it straight from the container.

You can't really see it but it's there, apparently. It doesn't bother us blokes though. We drink straight from the container all the time. Doesn't matter if it's orange juice, milk or tomato sauce. Why go to the trouble of tipping the sauce out and spreading it on your pie when you can just take a bite of your pie followed by a swig of the sauce from the bottle? Bite of the pie, swig of the sauce . . . bite, swig . . . and so on. It's far less messy. It shouldn't be about the backwash; it should be about blokes using our brains. We're just not given enough credit for our genius.

ballbreaker: a missus who gives you a hard time about everything.

When it gets to the stage where other people notice, then I'm afraid she's officially a ballbreaker. One of my mates no longer has any balls to speak of.

ballburster: a massive thumping kick so big it could have easily burst the ball.

In my heyday I was regarded as a great proponent of the ballburster. Sure, I had plenty of deficiencies in my game, but I could roost a ball a mile. My famous kick over the wheat silo at Mirrool was a ballburster.

banana: a shot for goal from an acute angle on the boundary line, which involves kicking the end of the ball so that in flight it bends like a banana.

Some South Australian commentators have infiltrated our game and tried to change it from a 'banana' to a 'checkside punt'. Wankers! We're sticking with banana and they can get stuffed.

> To **bank on** something means to rely on it. You need someone you can rely on to kick the winning goal after the siren, for example. You can bank on me — I'm Mr Reliable in that department.

bank: rip-off merchants.

They have fees for everything and no one to answer their phones. They've got most Australians by the short and curlies because we owe them heaps of money on our houses.

barbecue: blokes' cooking device.

Has its own set of specially designed tools. Never to be used by a woman. Ideal for burning sausages beyond recognition. Has caused numerous injuries due to faulty gas equipment combined with way too many beers. Anything less than a four-burner is embarrassing. Once it is no longer in perfect working order, it must be replaced immediately with a brand-new one, even if it means not paying other bills such as water, electricity, car servicing or school fees.

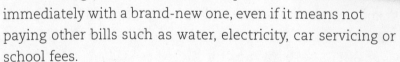

beep test: stupid, stupid fitness exercise designed by someone with a real hatred for humankind.

If you've never done it and hear it mentioned by your coach – run! Run for the hills!

beer: our best friend.

Unlike people, beer will never let us down. You've had a bad day? Beer will be there to comfort you. You've just finished a big job around the house? Beer will be there to reward you for your hard work. You're at a party where you don't know many people? Beer will be there to make you feel like someone cares about you. A mate drops by to say hello. Beer will be there to help you say to your mate, 'Thanks for coming around.' Throughout your life friends will come and go, but you can always grab a stubby of beer, hear that *pussst* noise as you twist off the bottle top, and as you take that first swig, think to yourself, 'Hello my good friend, you haven't changed a bit.'

bee's dick: unit of measurement, extremely small.

Not very complimentary towards bees.

bench: traditionally the worst position to be named in your football team.

Nowadays it's not as bad because often you'll start on the bench for tactical reasons and come on early. Later on in my career I became very familiar with the bench.

Berocca: a hangover cure.

Very important to always have some available. If not, I recommend an egg-and-bacon sandwich . . . fried.

⭐ **BFFL: best friends for life.**   TEENAGE SPEAK

Not to be confused with BFF – best friends forever.

⭐ **biatch: originally American gangster-rap speak now used by teenagers often as a lighter, less harsh version of 'bitch', but can still be used to show genuine disrespect towards someone else.**   TEENAGE SPEAK

Many, though, use it to refer to anybody. Billy says, 'Read on, biatches.'

Billy Brownless: legend (who put this in here?).

blast: what most coaches give the team when you're down at half time.
Blighty was the best there is at this. Just when you thought he'd peaked and run out of things to say, he'd take it up a notch and have you shuddering in your footy boots. I still maintain that I'm bald because his blasts blew most of my hair off.

bloke: a typical Australian male.
Me. I'm a bloke. Hopefully most of you are blokes. Kevin Rudd and Tony Abbott – not blokes. Only real blokes know what I mean by that.

blotto: really drunk.
Need to be carried home. Any more drunk and you'd be unconscious. We've all been blotto a few times in our lives. I have. There are two Geelong premierships that come to mind.

Bobby Davis: fair dinkum unbeliveable.

BO: body odour.
We all know someone who has bad BO. It's often someone we work with, hopefully not too closely. It's a difficult one to deal with and subtle hints are usually the way to go. A good trick is to leave a can of deodorant on their desk. When they see it, it should register with them; that is, of course, if they recognise what the hell it is.

BOG: best on ground.

Best player in a certain match. Doesn't just relate to a sporting field. Can also apply at a bar or nightclub. If one of your mates has done all right with the ladies at a particular venue, he can be awarded BOG.

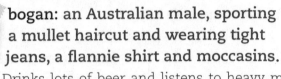

bogan: an Australian male, sporting a mullet haircut and wearing tight jeans, a flannie shirt and moccasins.

Drinks lots of beer and listens to heavy metal or rock music. We love bogans and tend to celebrate and embrace their image, mainly because we all have a bit of bogan in us. Bogans can also be female. They have a similar look to the male version, and in many cases have lots of children and can throw a stubby of beer with great accuracy. Considered very dangerous; do not approach.

boo: what the rest of the MCG does when the Mexican wave gets to the members.

Sometimes the members make a half-arsed effort to do the wave, which makes it look even worse. They may as well do nothing because they're going to get booed either way.

boobs: we all know what they are.

They come in all different shapes and sizes. We probably get a bit too excited about them. As teenage boys we'd giggle at the mere mention of them. As adult men we can't stop staring at them. We're not lecherous perverts, we're just showing our appreciation for some of God's great work. Could not possibly have a bloke's dictionary without this word in it.

boob-job: breast enlargement.

If you've read the previous definition, you'll understand why some women get this done. Just waiting for the technology to get to the point where it is of some use to us men. Not me, of course, just some blokes I know.

boofhead: idiot.

booty call: a special unwritten arrangement you have with a chick whereby you are not in a relationship but can call her at any time and hook up for sex only.

Often involving you popping in on your way home after a big night out. Unfortunately, this ideal situation never lasts. The arrangement can also work the other way.

botox: stuff that chicks (and Sam Newman) inject into their face to make them look younger.

Unfortunately, in most cases, it just makes them look scarier. This obsession with filling women's faces with a foreign substance is a real worry and needs to be stamped out pronto. It's hard enough as it is to work out what's upsetting the missus, so imagine how hard it'd be when she's got a face full of botox and you can't make out any expression at all.

bouncer: the bloke out the front of a nightclub or pub with a number on his jacket who doesn't let you in because you're not a hot chick.

They really should look after other blokes more than they do. Lucky most of them in Melbourne recognise my face, otherwise I'd have no chance of getting in anywhere. The industry is regulated now and all the bouncers must do a course on how to pummel the crap out of a drunk bloke who can hardly walk let alone fight back. Also the dog from *Neighbours*. One of

21

the only cast members not to release a single. He was on the show for six years, after which time I think he went to London to work the pantomime circuit.

brain freeze: the excuse most often used by me when I stuffed up on the footy field.
'Sorry, coach, I had a brain freeze . . . again.'

breasts: boobs.

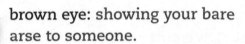

brown eye: showing your bare arse to someone.
Often done out of a car window. Spread your cheeks with your hands for the full effect.

brown nose: someone who sucks up to a person in a position of authority.
Very common in the workplace. Brown noses are quickly identified and then snubbed by their colleagues.

budgie smugglers: speedos. Brief bathers.
As worn by Tony Abbott. They leave nothing to the imagination. Should only ever be worn if you've got the body to go with them (like mine). Most blokes don't wear them and instead their preferred beach wear is one of the following: board shorts, footy shorts or even jeans. Blokes are also known to skinny dip if 1) drunk and 2) invited by a chick to do so.

bum crack: the part of your bum that sticks out above the waistband of your pants.
Very common among tradesmen, especially when they're

bending over (often referred to as plumber's crack or builder's crack). For some reason, it's not as sexy as when it's happening with a chick's bum.

bumfluff: facial growth that is very light and poor in its coverage.
Usually found on a teenage boy who is trying to grow his first beard. Basically looks like pubic hair on your face. Some blokes go through their entire lives only able to grow bumfluff.

burp: a loud noise made by blokes that really annoys chicks.
Usually accompanied by the smell of the previous meal mixed with beer. Some blokes practise their burps to the point where it's an art form. Those with real talent can burp on cue.

bushman's hanky: when a bloke places his thumb over one nostril while blowing out the other.
Some blokes are better at it than the rest. I suggest you spend time practising at home before doing it in public. If not done properly, it can get quite messy and you end up with snot down the front of your shirt. A very handy skill to have. It saves on hankies and can be done anywhere, any time. It is advised that you only do it outdoors.

C.C. Rider. Elvis used to start his concerts with that song. It was a beauty. Elvis reminds me a lot of myself. A good-looking superstar when he was young who let himself go a bit when he got older. I could shake my thing too, don't worry about that! In the end, he passed on and I had a hip replacement. In Roman numerals C stands for 100, which is what I used to tell my parents when I got a C for an assignment. Never really went down that well. One of my favourite 'C' things is CC's Corn Chips, which are great for dipping in stuff. I never know or even care what flavour dips are. Like most blokes, I just say, 'That green one tastes good and so does that light brown one.' I often Cc people in on emails. I never mean to, I usually just hit 'reply to all' by mistake. There's also the band 10cc – *'I don't like cricket'*. Here are some more C words that I promise not to sing.

cab: a taxi.

The ride you get home when you're drunk. Often difficult to hail in the city at 3 a.m. Never fall asleep in the cab because you'll arrive home to discover that the fare is twenty bucks more than you usually pay.

cabbie: someone who doesn't speak English, can't drive and has no idea what any of the streets are called or which is the best way to go.

cack: to have a laugh.

Also refers to defecating.

cack your pants: to lose control of your bowels and soil yourself due to being scared.

cack-hander: a left-hander.

cactus: ruined; wrecked.

Something is usually cactus after I've tried to fix it.

calorie: I'm not exactly sure what calories are or what they look like, but I do know that chicks like to count them.

I don't know where they find the time. As far as I'm concerned, when food is put in front of you, you eat it. Who's got time to work out how many calories it has and add that to those you had earlier in the day? By the time you've done that, the three donuts on the table have been eaten by the bloke sitting next to you.

Cameron Ling: superstar.

Geelong's favourite son. Blood nut.

can: a receptacle for storing beer.
Often carried in groups of six, a dozen or a slab. Kids or short people stand on them to get a better view at the footy. Also refers to a toilet: 'I need to go to the can.'

caning: a beating; an absolute spanking.
Can apply to sport. Many of my opponents would probably admit to copping a caning from me.

Captain Obvious: someone who says something that's generally accepted or understood by all.
Like if I'm walking down the street and someone yells out, 'Billy, you legend!' I always say, 'Good one, Captain Obvious.'

carby: a carburettor.

cardie: a cardigan.
Mainly worn by elderly blokes.

cark it: to die.
Can be used to refer to a person or a machine. 'The whipper snipper just carked it.'

carnie: someone who works at a carnival or theme park.
Those guys who jump on the back of your dodgem car to help you steer out of trouble when you are stuck against the edge. One of the jobs my school careers advisor said I would be suited to.

carpet burn: the most common injury sustained while playing indoor cricket.
It hurts slightly less if it is the result of a spectacular catch.

cashola: money, lots of it.
What Gary Ablett Jnr got to go to the Gold Coast.

Cats: the best team in the world.

CC and dry: Canadian Club whisky and dry ginger ale.
A good drink to move on to when you've had enough beer, which in my case is beer number 53.

cellulite: dimply skin, usually around the top of the legs and bum region.
Chicks are very sensitive about it, so don't point it out if you see it. If she mentions it herself, never ever admit to having noticed it.

cheap shot: having a go at someone by referring to something about them that they're not proud of.
You usually resort to cheap shots when you are losing an argument.

cheapie: an inexpensive product usually of inferior quality.

check-out chick: a girl who works behind the register at the supermarket.
They're very polite and always ask how I am, even though I'm sure deep down they don't really care whether I've had a shit day or not. These days, check-out chicks scan the barcodes on the groceries, so now they like to call themselves 'laser babes'.

HELLO
my name is
Chezza

chew the fat: to talk; to discuss stuff.
Blokes generally aren't very good at this.

chewie on ya boot: an expression yelled out to put someone off when they're lining up to have a shot for goal.
It has since been superseded by more personal remarks relating to nude photos that may have appeared on the internet.

chick: a female; girl; opposite to a bloke.
Blokes like chicks, chase chicks and hopefully, find one that likes them. You never refer to your wife as a chick.

chick magnet: a guy who attracts chicks because of his good looks.
He'll walk into a bar and chicks will literally throw themselves at him – but enough about me.

chin music: a bouncer.
A bowler might try to soften up a batsman with a little chin music. A tactic that was regularly used by my brothers in our backyard.

Chinese burn: a painful torture inflicted on a friend or younger brother where you twist the skin on their arm to the point where they feel a burning sensation.
You need two hands to do this as you need to twist the skin in opposite directions. There wouldn't be too many people who have grown up in this country and never been the victim of a Chinese burn. I'm pretty sure one of the main hospitals has a Chinese burns unit.

chip on their shoulder, has a: someone who has a problem or an issue with someone else.

chippie: a carpenter.

chock-a-block: packed; as full as something can be.
How I feel after I've eaten a meal or had a big night out on the frothies.

choof off: to leave; to go somewhere.

chucker: someone with an illegal bowling action, or someone who looks like they have an illegal bowling action but for some reason have been given the all-clear by the International Cricket Council.
I want to make it clear that I'm not referring to any particular player who may be from Sri Lanka and may have unfairly beaten Warnie's wicket-taking record. In the words of the crowd at the MCG, 'No ball!'

Chippies usually have tool belts. Get yourself one and you'll feel like the ultimate home handyman. But you might look like a real tool (see page 218).

chuck: spew; throw up; vomit.

chunder: spew; throw up; vomit.

When you **chuck / chunder / spew / vomit**, you often find yourself talking to the big white telephone.

clacker: a funny-sounding name for bum.
Always makes me laugh. Except when you have to have a colonoscopy and the doctor says he's going to put a tube with a camera on it up your clacker. There's no laughing then.

clanger: an embarrassing stuff-up.

It could be verbal or physical. Now an official AFL term for when a player makes a mistake. Thank God they weren't keeping a record of individual clangers when I played.

Man **cleavage** is making a comeback, apparently. You need to be very, very careful if you decide to go bare-chested. You could easily look like a dickhead (see page 39).

cleavage: that bit where a woman's breasts meet.

Often on display and hard to avert your eyes from. Chicks like to have it showing, but when you talk to them, they cover it up, even if you weren't looking. I get offended by that. I'm indirectly being accused of something I wasn't even doing. I once said to a woman that there was no need to cover up as I wasn't looking. Sure enough, as soon as she moved her hand I got caught looking. Didn't even realise I was doing it.

clip in the ear: to whack someone on the side of the head.

Dads used this to discipline their sons. Nowadays smacking is illegal, so it is mostly only used as a threat: 'You need a good clip in the ear!'

clown: an idiot; someone who has done something stupid.

I may have been called this once or twice.

cluey: smart; clever.

Can be used to refer to someone who knows a lot of stuff. Whoever commissioned me to write this book is very cluey.

Cocko: mate; pal; buddy.
My standard greeting. Maybe I should patent it. Read on, Cocko.

coco bananas: crazy; off ya nut; absolutely lost your shit.
A level often reached when the horse you backed gets pipped at the post.

 COD: Call of Duty. Video game.
Shoot 'em up big-time and play against others over the internet. I tried it and kept dying straightaway – soon realised I was holding the controls upside down.

coin jar: a jar in which you keep spare coins.
Often used for card money. Don't let your kids know where it is because no matter how many coins you put in there, it'll never fill up. My jar's still got two-cent pieces in it. Not sure what to do with them. I'm still hoping the government will have a change of heart and bring them back into circulation.

coldie: a cold can or stubby of beer.
 Beer must be cold. I've never heard anyone ask for a hottie.

collared shirt: what you need to wear to get into the members at the MCG.
You also need pants and shoes as well.

collywobbles: the nervous and shaky feeling you get when the pressure is on.

comfy: comfortable.

Commodore: a car made by Holden.
Often stolen to be used in bank robberies. They don't sponsor the Cats so this is all they get.

cooking with gas: to be doing really well; motoring along.
Like the Cats have been over the last five years.

cool: me.
What can I say? You all know it. Let's move on.

cop shop: a police station.
Where the Darl usually picks me up after a big night out. They've allocated her a car park now.

corporate box: a glassed-in room at the footy with a great view of the ground and free beer and food.
A trap for first-time users who, without fail, tend to get completely smashed and end up embarrassing themselves and the company they work for.

cougar: an older woman who chases younger men.
Something I had to deal with a lot when I was a strapping young recruit at Geelong. When I say older women, I mean older women. I was chased out of the Geelong car park once and the lady was pretty old. As fit as I was, there's only so long you can outrun one of those motorised scooters.

❀ **creep: any guy who thinks he is way cooler than he really is who's trying to pick up chicks.**
Creeps regularly hang out in bars, unaware that chicks are deliberately avoiding them. We need creeps because they make the rest of us look good.

cricket: something we used to be good at.
Now it's just embarrassing. We all took it for granted when Warnie, Oh Ah Glenn McGrath and Gilly were wreaking havoc. I wish I had enjoyed those wins more than I did. Now we have to listen to Poms mouthing off about beating us, and that hurts. As the saying goes, 'Old cricketers never die; they just go on to make hair-replacement ads.'

crikey: Steve Irwin's catchcry.
He was a great Australian who helped promote tourism and the protection of our wildlife. He was a real character who we all miss. His kids look as if they'll continue his work, so good on 'em!

crook: a criminal; someone who rips people off.
Also means 'feeling sick': 'I can't come because I'm a bit crook.'

crown jewels: testicles.
A bloke's most valuable assets. Must be protected at all times. I would hire a guard 24 hours a day if I could afford it.

Cup Day: a public holiday allocated for a horserace.
A day when people who know nothing about betting go down to the TAB and take up valuable space needed by us regular punters.

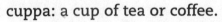

cuppa: a cup of tea or coffee.
Now there are so many versions of tea or coffee that it's become too confusing. People look at me strangely when I ask

for a plain and simple cup of coffee. I'm not sure anyone knows how to make one any more.

cushy job: a job where someone doesn't do much and still gets paid for it.
Like a politician. We've all got a mate with a cushy job, and we constantly remind him that he does bugger-all for a living.

cut someone's lunch: to make a move on someone else's girlfriend or a chick they're trying to pick up.
A big no-no in the world of blokes. Never ends well. Also referred to as 'cutting someone's grass'. Not to be confused with 'cutting the cheese', which means something completely different.

cutting the cheese: to fart.

35

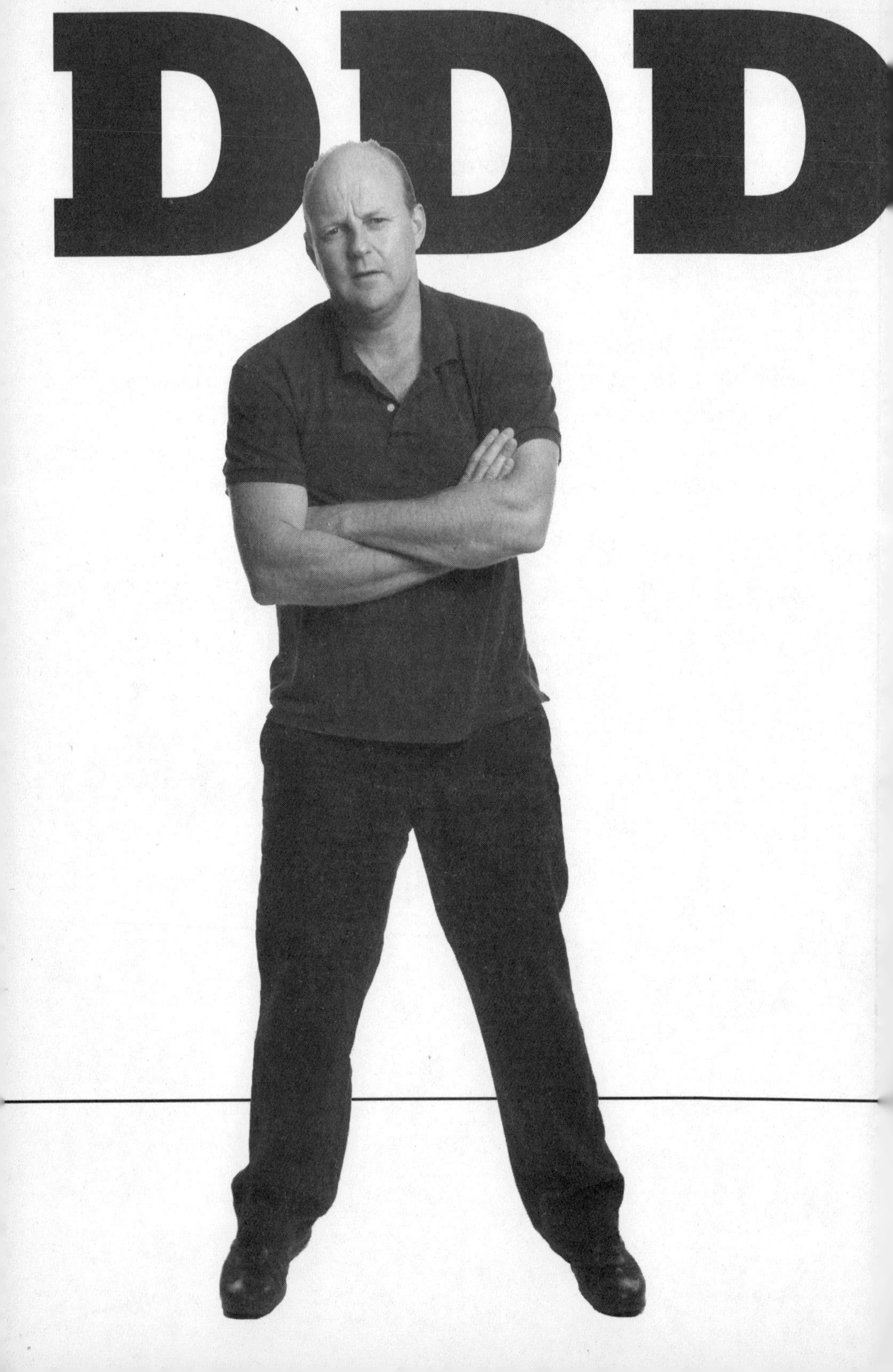
DDD

D is the fourth letter of the alphabet and, as we know, there are no medals for coming fourth. But let's not take anything away from D. D-day is one of the most important dates in military history. It was the day that Allied forces landed at Normandy on the French coast and began their march towards Germany to bring about an end to the Second World War. 3-D movies are all the rage at the moment. I've been to a few. Last time I went I forgot to take the glasses off and the drive home was in 3-D. One of our greatest ever comedy groups was the D-Generation. All in all, D has done pretty well. Let's have a look at some D words.

dack: to pull someone's pants down.

A great Australian pastime. For it to work well, it's very important you carefully sneak up on your mate. It's even more important to make sure that it is your mate you're sneaking up on. One of the easiest ways to dack a mate is when he's carrying beers back from the bar. He's never going to let the beers go, so he'll keep walking with his pants around his ankles until he can find somewhere to safely put the beers down.

Dad: father.

The person whose job it is to belittle you when you're growing up and embarrass you with their behaviour in front of your friends. Actions you vow never to repeat but end up doing to your own kids in exactly the same way.

Dad jokes: lame jokes dads tell their kids.

Kid: 'Dad, I'm hungry!'
Dad: 'Hi Hungry, I'm Dad.'
Nearly all my jokes fit the category of dad jokes.

damage: the cost of something that you're expecting to be expensive.

For example, when you get the bill for dinner: 'What's the damage?' Or when your girlfriend picks out the engagement ring she wants: 'Okay, what's the damage?'

Darl: the missus.

I told her she'd get a mention in the book and here it is.

dead-eye dick: someone who is a perfect shot.

They just don't miss. Like me in front of goal to win a preliminary final. *Yes!! Go, Billy!!*

dead horse: rhyming slang for tomato sauce.
Probably the most commonly used rhyming slang we have. It doesn't seem to want to go away.

dead-set legend: someone who is, without doubt, a legend.
G. Ablett.

Dead horse on pie. My two favourite food groups in one bite. Perfection.

dead wood: people who are of no use but are still hanging around.
'We need to get rid of the dead wood.'

decked out: how someone is dressed.
Right now, as I write this, I'm decked out in some undies and a singlet. Trust me, I make it look good.

derr: the sound you make when someone has said something obvious.
For example, 'Gary Ablett Jnr must've been named after his Dad.' – 'Derrr!'

desperado: a bloke who is hanging around chicks at a bar and not taking the hint that they don't want him there.
If this is you, it may be time to consider hanging up the boots.

dickhead: an idiot.
Often yelled out during road rage: 'Watch where you're going, dickhead!' Sometimes it can be said in a more lighthearted fashion: 'Geez, you're a dickhead, Barry.'

digger: a returned soldier. Massive respect.

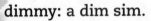

dimmy: a dim sim.

Chinese dumpling-style snack. Can be steamed or fried. Typically served with soy sauce. Always goes down well with a hangover. Amazingly, if someone has just eaten a dim sim you can smell them coming from two suburbs away. Not many of you would know this but the dimmy was invented in 1945 in Melbourne by Chinese chef William Wing Young for his restaurant Wing Lee. He used to sell them at the footy and before too long his factory was producing them by the thousands. On behalf of all Australians, I say thank you William Wing Young. The dimmy is an Aussie icon. Who wants a couple right now? Me!

dinger: a condom.

As a young man, you always carried one in your wallet. Often it was in there for so long that it left a round imprint visible from the outside. Not a good look.

dink: to give someone a lift on your bike.

Very popular with teenagers. You can either put the person on the handlebars or sit them on the crossbar. Having them on the handlebars makes for really heavy steering and having them on the crossbar makes pedalling a bit cramped. The advantage to both methods of dinking is that you have someone to break your fall if you stack.

dirty weekend: when you go away for the weekend with your girlfriend or wife.

Doesn't matter where you go, there'll always be a mate nudging you in the ribs, saying, 'Dirty weekend, hey!' To be honest, it usually is dirty. Me and the Darl end up arguing, and she dirties up.

dishlicker: a greyhound.

If you're at the TAB and you start betting on the dogs, then it's

time to go home, I reckon. At least horses have a human on top to steer and tell them when to go fast. Billy's tip: when in doubt, back the red dog.

dive: a dirty, messy place.
Often used to describe a bar or nightclub. Not that it stops blokes from going there. 'To dive' also means to exaggerate a fall. Soccer players have perfected this, as have a couple of full-forwards.

divvy van: a police divisional van used to transport people who have been arrested.
When they have someone handcuffed in the back, the police tend to take the corners a bit sharper. Used in one of the classic chants at the cricket, following someone's arrest: *'You're going home in the back of a divvy van!'*

dobber: someone who tells on someone else.
No one likes a dobber, especially when you're at school.

dodgy: dishonest; crooked.
A deal that is too good to be true. Guys selling speakers out of a white van on the side of the street. If those guys happen to be reading this, I want my money back, thanks.

doggie style: when the Western Bulldogs win in style.
Yes, I know it means something else, but do I really need to explain it?

Doggies: the Western Bulldogs.
Everyone's second-favourite team. Joined the league in 1925 and have won only one premiership, in 1954. Surely, they're due one soon. They may have to wait till after the AFL arrange one for the Gold Coast and Greater Western Sydney teams.

dog's breakfast: a mess.
Any room I happen to be staying in. Apologies to any dogs that
are quite neat when it comes to their breakfasts.

**Don Bradman: the greatest sportsman Australia
has ever produced.**
He averaged a remarkable 99.94 in test cricket and used
to practise by hitting a golf ball into a water tank with a
cricket stump. He is now in a glass case in the museum . . . no,
hang on, that's Phar Lap. My mistake.

donkey: my nickname.

donnybrook: a fight.
But more of your fun sort of fight, where no one really gets hurt.

**Dorothy Dixer: a question that is worded in such a
way that the person can only give the answer the
interviewer wants.**
It is traditionally used by politicians, who set someone up to
ask a question in parliament so that they look impressive
when they give their answer. Dorothy Dix was an American
advice columnist with a reputation for making up her own
questions so that she could write more interesting answers.
Gee, how did you know all that, Billy? I'm a genius who does
his research. There you go, a Dorothy Dixer.

dosh: money.

**double or nothing: the first thing we say after losing
a bet with someone to avoid having to pay them.**
We stand to lose twice as much as the original bet but we
don't care. We just don't want to cough up the money there
and then.

down the hatch: an expression you use when you're about to pour a beer down your throat.
A bit harder to say after you've done it about 15 times.

Down Under: Australia.
How America likes to refer to us. Made famous by the Men at Work song, which is our unofficial anthem. Well, that and 'Am I Ever Gonna See Your Face Again?' You know the rest.

downsizing: the excuse companies use for retrenching their workers.
In other words, downsizing means trying to increase the company's profit. After you have been retrenched, you can always downsize the tyres on the boss's car.

drill: a tool for drilling holes in something.
Feels great in your hands and makes a good noise. The drill is my favourite tool, unless it belongs to a dentist.

drive-thru: what the fast-food people introduced to make it even easier for us to eat their food.
Great idea. We don't even have to get out of our car to order. The only problem is when you don't get the car close enough to the window for a smooth enough handover. You're reaching out. The girl is at full stretch, trying to hand you the food. You can't back up and then drive closer to the window because there's a queue of cars behind you. You're scared that the girl will drop the food and it'll be lost forever. Eventually, you make the exchange and breathe a sigh of relief. Trying to eat it while you're driving is another challenge altogether. There's nothing worse than taking a bite out of your rather tasteless burger only to realise that the insides are now sitting in your lap and

leaving a very embarrassing stain on your jeans. I once got to the speaker thingo in the drive-thru and spent five minutes ordering before the guy in the car behind me yelled out, 'Hey, mate. You're talking into the rubbish bin!'

drop a bombshell: to make an announcement that stuns everyone.

I've dropped some bombshells in my time. Most of them were later proven to be false, which was a bit unfortunate for those people involved. Ah, well, a bit late now.

drop kick: a kick that was once very prominent in footy but is now extinct.

Also refers to someone who is a bit of an idiot.

dry area: an area without alcohol.

What sort of drop kick came up with that?

duffer: someone who has stuffed up, usually in a minor way.

It's more of a supportive go at someone. They might knock over a drink and you would say, 'You're a bit of a duffer, but never mind.' It can't really be applied to more serious stuff-ups. For example, you wouldn't call the Captain of the *Exxon Valdez*, which struck a reef and spilled crude oil along miles of coastline, a duffer.

duffle coat: a big woollen coat with a hood and wooden toggles for buttons.

Very popular at the footy in the '60s and '70s. Supporters would put a player's number on the back and team badges on the sleeves and on the front. It's a pity they went out of fashion because no one had the chance to wear my number.

dummy spit: when someone chucks a wobbly, big time.
Often seen in sport. John McEnroe was one of the best dummy spitters of all time. It's safe to abuse the umpire in tennis. He's way up high in that chair. By the time he climbs down to have a go back, you're already out of there.

dunno: the answer you give to any question that, if answered truthfully, could get you into trouble.
'Who left that dirty plate on the table?' – Dunno. 'How did that hole get in the wall?' – Dunno. 'What happened to that vase my mum gave me?' – Dunno. The missing vase and the hole in the wall were actually connected, but don't tell the Darl.

duster monitor: the best job to have at school.
You would get a ruler and just bash the chalk dust out of the duster. These days they have whiteboards and so that job has become obsolete. Young people no longer get to experience the joy of whacking the duster while at the same time filling their lungs with heaps of chalk dust. After school you'd struggle to walk to the car without having to stop because you were coughing up puffs of chalk.

dust-up: a fight.
But a fairly tame fight where no one gets hurt. If you find yourself in a bar fight, it's important to make sure the other people involved understand that it's only a dust-up and not a full-on fistfight. You don't want anyone getting hurt.

Dutch oven: farting under the doona and then pulling the doona over your missus' head, so that she cops the full force of your fine work.
She never seems to get the joke. I assume it was a Dutchman who first tried it. How's that? They're known for windmills, clogs, tulips and a fart prank.

E has become a super-popular letter thanks to the internet. Heaps of businesses based on the net start with the letter e. The most famous being eBay, where some of you may have bought this book or even tried to sell it – having got so much enjoyment out of it, you thought it only fair that someone else should get to experience it. Good on you, I say. Bruce Springsteen had the E Street band; I have an e-TAG in my car for driving where there are tolls; I hire DVDs from Video Ezy, and I like watching Ernie Els – or as he is affectionately known, the Big Easy – play golf. Do you want more E? I know you do.

Eagles: West Coast Eagles.

Western Australian team with massive support, a couple of premierships and a tarnished reputation for off-field behaviour.

If you **earbash** someone, chances are they'll start yawning. That's your cue to shut up. If you look at this picture for long enough you'll start yawning. Sorry about that, I'll shut up now.

earbash: to tell someone off or talk too much to the one person for an extended period of time; a boring conversation with someone that goes on and on and on.

A lot of earbashers don't even realise that they're doing it. Maybe I'm doing it to you right now. I couldn't be sure. Does it feel like you're getting an earbashing because if it does, I'll stop. Should I stop? Not sure if I should stop. Okay, I'll keep going. No, all right, I'll stop. Stopping now. There, I've stopped. I've come to a halt. Never thought I would, to be honest. I'm doing it again, aren't I?

earshot: the range in which something can be heard.

Whenever a coach asked me why I didn't follow the instructions he'd yelled across the ground, I'd always say that I wasn't in earshot. Unfortunately, I was always within throwing distance and would usually cop something in the head as punishment.

easy on the eye: something or someone that is good to look at.

Like the Darl. Sure, there are possibly a few other women who are easy on the eye, but I've only ever looked at them briefly, I promise. There are probably guys out there who women find easy on the eye and I could be one of them.

easy-peasy: something that can be done with minimal effort.

Like me playing football – easy-peasy. Except for the training part. That was hardey-wardey.

effing: replacement for the f-word.

You can sound and feel like you're swearing without even swearing. It doesn't get any effing better than that. I'm starting to have an effing good time writing this book now. Ah, this is the effing life.

el cheapo: anything that is not only cheap in value but also in quality.

We often justify buying something that's el cheapo because we think it will do for a short period of time. Usually when it breaks, we say, 'Ah, well, it was only an el cheapo.' There are a couple of no-nos when it comes to buying el cheapo stuff. I'd never buy el cheapo tools, furniture, cars or condoms and I'd never, ever fly with an el cheapo airline.

elbow grease: hard work.

'Put a bit of elbow grease into it!' Dads are usually saying this to their kids when they get them to help out around the house. As a kid, I only put in elbow grease when it was something I enjoyed, like getting ready to go to the tip. If Dad wanted me to do something boring like sand something back for painting, I was all out of elbow grease. If only you could pop down to the hardware store and buy a whole tin of elbow grease.

Your funny bone is right near your **elbow**, but it's a nerve not a bone. A funny bone is one of the best things you could have up your sleeve. That's almost a Dad joke (see page 38).

elbow room: the space you have to work in.

There could be a lot of elbow room or very little. Running around on the footy field, there was plenty of elbow room. Unfortunately, you weren't allowed to use them.

Elvis: The King.

This mantle now belongs to Wayne Carey, who can't sing or play the guitar. Elvis was a trailblazer, who made it okay for blokes to party, eat greasy food and bed a lot of women. That was until he died at the young age of 42. Then everyone realised that maybe it wasn't the way to go. It didn't stop most of us giving it a crack, though.

emcee: master of ceremonies.

The person whose job it is to host a function and introduce other speakers. I've done a lot of emcee-ing in my time, especially down at Geelong. Pretty sure they've heard all my jokes about 100 times. When the audience starts reciting your stories one sentence ahead of you, it's time for some new material.

emo: someone who has dyed-black hair, wears black nail polish and skin-tight black pants and listens to a particular type of music.

`·TEENAGE SPEAK·`

Most of them grow out of it, thankfully.

empties: empty beer bottles, stubbies and/or cans.

After a party, it's always amazing where you find empties. I have found them in the letterbox, in the dryer, inside my pillowcase. Once I even found one in, of all places, the recycling bin. I couldn't believe someone had bothered to do that. It was not only thoughtful but the walk out to the bins would've cost them at least two minutes of their drinking time. As a kid I used to volunteer to stack Dad's empties behind the shed. I did this for two reasons: 1) You could be very creative with your stacking and 2) each stubby had enough left in it for a little swig. The more swigs I had, the worse I'd stack.

end-over-end kick: what the American commentators call a 'drop punt' when it's done by an NFL punter.

Australian punters playing in the US started doing it because it was a good kick to do when you needed a high short punt. We invented the kick in Aussie Rules and it's called a 'drop punt', so stop calling it an end-over-end kick, you idiots.

enough said: an expression used to stop a discussion.

'Don't argue with me; let's just leave it at that.' Any questions? Enough said.

esky: a device for keeping beer cool.

Sure, it keeps other stuff cool as well, like meat, salads and cordial, but if you're running out of room, the beer takes priority. Can also be used as a chair, unless it's one of those foam eskies, or as we called them, 'the kick to death esky'. I sat on one of those once and totally obliterated it.

even keel, on a: trying to keep things balanced.

Steady as she goes. When I've got a beer in one hand and a packet of chips in the other, Billy's on an even keel.

even stevens: equal.

If you win one and your opponent wins one, then you are even stevens. If you're playing tennis and it's one-set all, it's even stevens. I was once even stevens with my mate Steven, which made it really confusing.

every dog has its day: eventually everybody has their chance at success.

I kept telling myself that when we lost four grand finals. Although, I changed it to 'every cat has its day', which is probably why it didn't work.

every man and his dog: a lot of people.

Every man and his dog turned up to Kardinia Park the day after the Cats won the 2007 Grand Final. I feel bad now that I didn't take mine. Then again, I hadn't been home.

evil eye: what your wife or girlfriend gives you when they're not happy.

Don't stare back at it for too long because it might kill you. Sometimes you're given the evil eye and you're not even sure why. You just stare back, looking a bit confused. That's when she somehow takes the evil eye up a notch and it becomes even more piercing. It's at that point that you need to work out what you've actually done because if you give in and ask what you've done, you get another look altogether that makes you feel sick in the tummy. Blokes try to give the evil eye but we can't do it anywhere near as well as chicks.

excuse the French: what someone says after swearing, as if to apologise.

I was never sure why we compare it to speaking French. So when I was in France, I walked into a restaurant and started swearing my head off. The waiter seemed to understand everything I said. He got me the best table by the window and I had a great meal. Before leaving I swore at him again and he smiled and got my coat for me.

extract the digit: to start working after a period of laziness.

A boss will often tell one of their workers to extract the digit if they haven't been working hard enough. We obviously don't overwork in this country. I've never heard a boss say, 'Insert the digit.'

eye-opener: something you've seen that has given you an insight.

Spending a game in the coach's box would be a real eye-opener. Not sure they'd ever let me in there, though. Well, I know they wouldn't. I knocked on the door during a game once and they all hid behind their chairs, pretending they weren't there. I felt like a Mormon knocking on someone's front door.

F has a bad reputation due to its regular use in the f-word. Unfairly so, I say. Let's be honest, we all use the f-word, so the letter F is a lot closer to our hearts than we would like to admit. So, don't be embarrassed by F; let's celebrate and embrace it. Imagine where we'd be without it. It's always there for us when we need it. Without F, what would we yell out when we hit our thumb with a hammer or lock the keys in the car? Where would we be without F when our footy team loses by a point on the siren? What would we do without F when someone cuts us off on the road? Are you with me? See what I mean? Yes, I love F too.

face plant: when someone falls and lands on their face in a way that makes everyone watching cringe – and then laugh, of course.

I know my face looks like I've landed on it a few times but I haven't.

Facebook: a social-networking website.

People give status updates, upload photos, write on walls and chat. Some blokes successfully maintain a Facebook page, others have struggled to get involved. I say, each to his own on this one. Personally, I don't have time to do all that stuff. I'll leave it up to the fake Billy Brownless. I've seen the page. He's out there. I haven't got a problem with someone getting their kicks pretending to be me, as long as they're prepared to share the load in other ways as well. I'm not asking too much. You know, maybe pick up the kids from school once in a while or mow the lawns, that's all.

Fair go — when Kev said, 'fair shake of the sauce bottle' it was probably his dinnertime and the sauce bottle was nearly empty, so he was shaking it to get the last drops out. What's dinner without a bit of dead horse (see page 39), even in the Lodge?

fair go: a plea to give someone a chance.

A very Aussie thing to promote, and something we see as an important rule to follow. Everyone deserves a fair go. I often said this to opponents who were towelling me up in a game. Unfortunately, not many were willing to come to the party.

fair suck of the sauce bottle: give me a go; a plea for fair treatment.

In an interview, then-Prime Minister Kevin Rudd got the saying wrong when he said, 'Fair shake of the sauce bottle'. Thankfully he didn't attempt any other well-known

Aussie sayings, otherwise we may have heard stuff like this: 'Come on, mate, put your mummy where your mouth is!' or 'Chewie on your boob!'

fairweather supporter: one who only follows their team when they're winning.

Nowhere to be seen when the team is going through a bad patch. These supporters don't say anything to anybody at work for most of the footy season, but when their team wins they come out of the woodwork and give everyone else the shits.

fake tan: chicks like to put this on before a big occasion.

I'm not sure why it is so important that they need to look orange, but sometimes you'd think they'd been rolling around in a vat of pumpkin soup. Don't get me wrong, I like pumpkin soup but I wouldn't wear it out. Girls, it's called fake tan for a reason – it looks fake! It also smells a bit weird.

Fanta pants: a redhead; Cameron Ling.

Obviously, if someone has red hair on their head, they will have it everywhere else, including in their pants. Having actual Fanta in your pants isn't much fun, as I can attest to after I purchased some meal deals from the Macca's drive-thru and had the Fanta tip over in my lap. It's true what they say – ice does reduce the swelling.

Farnsy: John Farnham.

Legend of the Australian music industry. Also owner of one of the best mullets ever. A truly great Australian. If only I had hair and could sing, we'd have a lot in common.

fart: a sound emitted from one's bum that is usually accompanied by an unpleasant smell.

Often referred to in the following ways: cut the mustard, drop ya guts, who opened the lunch box?, who let rip? and Vince. I can't believe I had to sit down and write a definition for 'fart', and then send it to the publisher for their approval. I think I nailed it, though.

Gross!

(see page 74)

fart jar: a glass jar that is passed around at school for people to fart into.

After each fart, the lid is quickly put back on so that the fart can't escape. I was always a bit suss on whether the fart jar actually worked, but I soon realised it did after it was shoved under my nose during English one day. It knocked me off my chair and I was subsequently sent to the Principal's office. The jar was eventually put in the recycling bin. Hope it isn't now being used for jam.

fast buck, to make a: to earn money with little effort.

Often involving a dodgy scheme of some sort. So, if you know of one, give me a call. I had a crack at that aeroplane pyramid thing that did the rounds in the '80s. You put in $1000 and try to make it all the way up to pilot. I ended up chucking a parachute on and jumping out of there.

fat chance: no chance at all.

When I retired, they said I had a fat chance of getting a game. I'm not sure but I think they were giving the term 'fat chance' a double meaning there.

feathers: a bloke's plumage.
Something I don't have a lot of.

feed the chooks: to stretch the truth.
Behave like a bit of a wanker. Also means to actually feed the chooks because if you don't feed them, you know what happens? That's right – no more KFC and I wouldn't be able to survive.

fell off the back of a truck: stolen goods.
When you get offered something at a price that is too good to be true, you always suspect that it fell off the back of a truck. The phrase was coined by the people selling dodgy items as a way of explaining where they got the goods from. I think my fridge fell off the back of a truck. It's got a big dent in it.

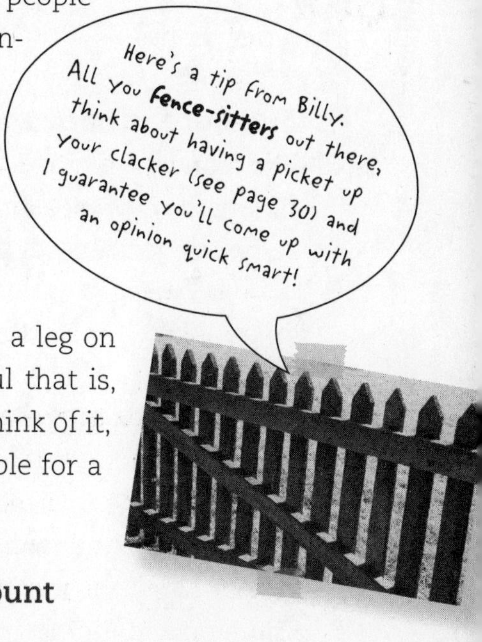

fence-sitter: someone who won't take a side in an argument.
They prefer to 'sit on the fence' with a leg on either side, and we know how painful that is, especially if you're a bloke. Come to think of it, I can't imagine it being too comfortable for a woman either.

Here's a tip from Billy. All you **fence-sitters** out there, think about having a picket up your clacker (see page 30) and I guarantee you'll come up with an opinion quick smart!

fiddle the books: to alter the account books of a business.
It could be done in an effort to fool the taxman or make the business sound a lot better than it is, so that you can sell it. It makes me sound like I've done it before but let me tell you, I haven't. The taxman can never be fooled for too long and besides, I pay my taxes, so why shouldn't everyone else. Most businesses now keep their books on computer, so the saying

may need to change in order to cater for future generations, who won't even know what books are.

filthy: angry; upset about something that has happened.

Fortunately, I don't get filthy very often because I'm too much of an easygoing sort of bloke. If I did filthy up, I doubt anyone would take me seriously anyway.

filthy look: what the Darl gives me when I stumble through the front door after a few frothies.

I got the worst filthy look ever when I stumbled through the front door last week. Then again, I had stumbled into the wrong house.

find out the hard way: to learn from your mistakes.

The standard method of teaching employed by most fathers. I think they get pleasure out of seeing their sons suffer. 'Dad, I think I've accidentally cut off my finger.' 'That'll learn ya, son!'

fish and chips: one of the greatest meals ever invented.

Fish and chips are an important part of my diet. I'm usually on a seafood diet — when I see food, I eat it. That's another Dad joke (see page 38).

A staple for many families on a Friday night. They're cooked while you wait, and that twenty minutes of sitting in the shop seems to go for an hour. The anticipation of waiting for your number to be called out is almost unbearable. When they finally yell it out, the relief is amazing. The fish-and-chip guy gets a big hug from me every time. He must really enjoy it because he's always slipping in a couple of extra potato cakes.

fishy: dodgy; something that is suspicious.
Like a guy coming up to me in the street and offering me Rolex watches at a really cheap price. Probably shouldn't have bought seven of them. Three still work, though.

fixed: a sporting event where the result has been prearranged.
For example, most of the horseraces I've lost money on.

fizzer: a dud; a failure; an event that doesn't go well.
I've never been to a party that was a fizzer. Probably because I was there, hey?

flake: a shark fillet.
Very popular on the fish-and-chip-shop menu. No wonder sharks are attacking us. We're eating all of their relatives. They're just trying to redress the balance. Also means to pass out, especially after a few beers. The last time I flaked it, I tried to pass it off as a nanna nap. Problem was, it was a fourteen-hour nanna nap.

flash, not too: below standard.
For example, 'I can't mow the lawn today Darl, I'm not feeling too flash.'

flasher: someone who exposes their private parts in public.
They are then somehow surprised to discover that no one is really that interested in seeing their bits, which must be disappointing.

flashy: showy, pretentious, up yourself.
Not me – I'm much better than that.

flat chat: going as fast as one can.

Never something I experienced on the training track. That was until they'd call an end to training, at which point I would somehow find a burst of speed to enable me to get into the showers first.

flicks: the movies.

I don't get to the flicks as much as I'd like. I must admit that I still prefer getting a DVD because you can pause it at any time so that you can work out what the hell is going on or because it's that scene with Sharon Stone in *Basic Instinct*.

fling: a brief relationship with someone.

Often refers to an affair. I've been married to the Darl for years but she still refers to it as a fling – or does that make it a 3768-night stand?

flour bomb: a paper bag full of flour that is thrown at someone in fun or to ridicule them.

The paper bag explodes on impact, covering the victim in flour. A popular weapon for teenagers but you can still get a lot of joy out of them as an adult. Go on, I'll give you five minutes now to make one and chuck it at someone. You can come back to reading this later. Go! This book's not going anywhere.

fluke: when you do something spectacular by accident.

Remember when I kicked that goal after the siren to put us into the preliminary final? Yeah? Well, that *wasn't* a fluke, all right! I meant it, and if I hear another person telling me that it was a fluke, there's a good chance they could somehow fluke their way through the closest window.

foggiest, I don't have the: having no idea.
Regularly used by me when I'm driving somewhere and am struggling to work out where I am. In the end I had to buy a GPS. Unfortunately, that gets me lost as well, yet it never admits it is lost. Just once I would like to hear it say, 'I wouldn't have the foggiest where you are.'

folding: cash money in notes.
I once asked my nanna if she had any folding, and she handed me the washing off the line.

footing the bill: when one person pays for the entire bill.
When parents pay to put their kids through school, or pay for their kids' birthday parties or even their weddings. Shit, I'd better start saving!

footy smarts: having a good brain for playing footy.
Nothing to do with IQ (see page 93).

fox: hot chick.
They never really appeared to be that interested in me, which I took as them playing hard to get. Yep, I was wrong.

Frank Costa: ex-Geelong President, who led the club to the long-awaited 2007 and 2009 premierships.
He needs to be given credit for the role he played in turning the Cats back into a force to be reckoned with. By keeping our home games in Geelong, he has ensured a financially rewarding future for the club. He also runs a very successful fruit business. I'm not that familiar with fruit, but it's supposed to be good for you.

Fred Hollows: an ophthalmologist (eye doctor), who became famous for restoring eyesight to thousands of underprivileged people in Australia and around the world.

They reckon that more than a million people can now see because of the organisation he set up (The Fred Hollows Foundation). He was named Australian of the Year in 1990. He must've just pipped me at the post for that one.

French kissing: when you kiss and stick the tongue in.

It can be great but it can also bring about your downfall. I suggest you use it sparingly. Too much tongue darting in and out can get really annoying for the other person. Less is better, I say. Yep, I'm an expert on kissing too. I was voted best pasher at school. Sure, it was an all-boys school but you've got to take your trophies where you can get them.

Freo: Fremantle.

Nice place. Fair way to go for me but always worth it.

frothy: a beer.

My favourite way of saying my favourite drink. It somehow makes getting drunk sound pretty harmless, especially when you're trying to explain your intoxicated state to the Darl. 'I've only had a couple of frothies.'

fruit loop: someone who is unhinged, crazy.

I may have met a few of these types over my time in football and in the media. I'm not going to mention any names for fear of repercussions, especially from some very close friends of mine and ex-teammates, but I do wonder what John Barnes is up to these days.

full: drunk.

full as a boot: drunk.

full as a fat lady's sock: drunk.

full as a goog: drunk.
Also used when you've had more than enough to eat. So when your mother-in-law offers you thirds, you can say, 'No thanks, I'm full as a goog.'

full as a tick: drunk.

full of yourself: in love with yourself.
That's one thing I can never be accused of, which might surprise a few people because I'm incredibly handsome and talented.

I can't think of the letter G without immediately thinking of Geelong (the footy team) and Geelong (the city). And then, of course, G. Ablett. I played with Gazza, and we all know what a superstar he was, but Gary Junior has managed to prolong the greatness associated with the name. The person who has got the most joy out of it would have to be AFL supremo Andrew Demetriou. How much does he love sitting on that G when he reads it out on Brownlow night? 'Geelong, three votes, G. . . . *pause . . . pause . . . keeps pausing . . . Billy goes to the toilet, comes back after having a chat with someone on the way . . . still pausing . . .* Ablett.' G is a very significant letter in my life. I say 'geez' a lot, I like to punt on the gee-gees, and I've been known to wear the odd G-string. Sometimes, I do all three at once. More G below.

G and T: gin and tonic.

A good 'go-to' drink when you're not sure what you want. You probably wouldn't start with it, especially if you're out with your mates. It's not considered the manliest of drinks. You need to suss out your group before deciding whether it's okay to order one.

Gabba: Queensland cricket ground.

Also the home of the Brisbane Lions. You know, I still hold the record for the most goals kicked at the Gabba. It's eleven. Each year I sneak up there and move the goalposts a bit closer together to protect my record. The Gabba is actually named after the suburb of Woolloongabba.

I used to think that the Gabba was an acronym that stood for something, like with the MCG (Melbourne Cricket Ground). I spent ages trying to work it out. For years I was convinced 'Gabba' stood for the 'Great Arena Brisbane Bogans Attend'. Then again, maybe I was right.

> Galahs are Aussie birds that make a helluva lot of noise. Like I said, they probably shouldn't be running the country.

⭐ GAL: get a life.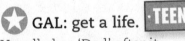
Usually has 'Dad' after it.

galah: an idiot; someone who acts the fool.

Most of them end up taking the same path in life – becoming a politician.

game on: what you say when you take up a challenge.

The reply you give when a one-on-one competition has

been suggested by a competitor. Also said when someone plays a practical joke on you and you want to get them back: 'Okay, then, game on!' I like saying 'game on' to people even if they haven't said anything to me. It really confuses them.

garbage guts: someone who eats anything and everything.

They'll just keep tipping food into their mouths, often shovelling it down their throat at a really fast rate. Hang on, why does this all sound so familiar?

garbo: a person who collects garbage.

Technology has seen their job change dramatically. When I was a kid, there would be four garbos hanging off the side of a truck as it came down the street. They'd jump off at each house, pick up the tin garbage bin and tip the contents into the back of the truck. They'd make heaps of noise as bins were grabbed, banged together and then thrown back, only to end up three houses down from where they were supposed to be. Now it's just the one garbo driving the truck, which has mechanical arms to pick up the bins. The garbo gets really angry when a car is parked too near the bin, and the truck's mechanical arm can't reach it. He has to get out of the truck to move the bin to a spot that suits the truck. The pissed-off look on his face is pretty funny, which is why I keep parking the car in front of the bin. Some days I'll fill the bin up with bricks to make it even harder to move. It's hilarious.

gastro: the most commonly used excuse when ringing in sick to get a day off work.

It's perfect because gastro only lasts 24 hours. You can walk into work the next day looking good and no one will ask any questions. Now, by no means do I want to encourage all the readers of this book to take a day off, especially if you all do it tomorrow. At least spread it out over a couple of days so that people don't get suss. Anyway, ring each other up and work it out.

gatecrash: turning up to a party uninvited.
Some teenagers make the mistake of putting the details of their party on Facebook for anyone to see. Nothing worse than 400 people turning up when you've only made enough fairy bread for 35.

gawk: to stare; to look at someone without hiding the fact.
The person you're staring at will often get angry and say, 'What are you gawking at?' Try lining up for goal in a final with 90 000 people gawking at you. I kicked the goal, by the way, just in case you were wondering.

gee-gees: race horses.
Some of which I may bet on from time to time. Just every now and again, of course. Nothing I can't control. *Go, you good thing!*

get a grip: to pull yourself together; have a reality check.
If something minor has caused you to get angry or upset, someone will often tell you to 'get a grip'. Not sure what you grip exactly, so I guess you just grab whatever is closest.

girly mag: a magazine with pictures of naked women in it.
Very popular among teenage boys, many of whom get caught reading one in class hidden behind their maths textbook. The teacher then confiscates it and you never see it again. One of my teachers ended up with the best collection of girly mags

in the country. I reckon he took long service leave just to give himself enough time to get through them all.

glass jaw, to have a: to be knocked out easily on a regular basis.

Not many people know this but I once put Gary Ablett Snr on his bum during a boxing-training session at Geelong. Sure, it was a lucky punch and I would love to take it back because the look in his eye when he finally got to his feet was enough for me to ditch the gloves and immediately head off on foot. I was setting a cracking pace and was halfway to Melbourne before a Geelong fan pulled up and offered me a lift back.

glass someone: to smash a glass into someone's face.

Thanks to idiots who have done this in the past, a lot of pubs now serve beer in plastic glasses. I'm not sure how I can call them 'plastic glasses'; they're either one or the other but you know what I mean. Anyway, what an outrage it is that we now have to drink beer out of plastic. I refuse, point-blank, to drink at a pub that uses plastic glasses. Unless, of course, it's a fair drive to the next pub and I can't wait. Who am I kidding? Let's face it: I'd drink beer out of a sock if that was all that was available. Come to think of it, I think I did drink beer out of Paul Chapman's footy sock after the Cats won the flag in '07.

go at it hammer and tongs: to have a real crack at something.

Put everything into it. Can refer to a fight or a couple going for it in the bedroom. Personally, I don't think a hammer or tongs should be anywhere near the bedroom but each to their own.

goer: someone who has a dip; one who's very keen to have a crack.
A couple of kids who came down to Geelong in my time were real goers. Didn't have my talent, of course, but good on them for trying. Can also refer to an event that is going ahead. 'That boys' day at the races is a goer.' 'That boys' golf day is a goer.' 'The poker night is a goer.' Okay, you're on to me. I'm now just using this book to get some messages out to my mates.

going over, a: having a close look at something.
If you're buying a car, you might get someone to give it a good going over before you pay for it. I wish I had done that when I bought one of my first cars. Maybe they would've picked up that it was an old taxi. Then again, the fact that it was yellow and stunk inside was a bit of a giveaway.

golden duck: going out on the first ball you face in cricket.
This always results in a pretty embarrassing walk back to the pavilion. It's hard enough to live down in the backyard or in local cricket, so I can only imagine what it must feel like at test level to have to trudge off in front of 90000 people. I once went out for a golden seagull. I was at the beach and the first ball I faced I hit into a seagull and then one of my mates caught it with one hand. I felt so bad for the seagull that I let him have a bat later.

golden handshake: money given to an employee who has been forced into retirement.
I must've missed out on that somehow. In those days you got the golden boot up the bum.

gonads: testicles.

A lot of indoor cricket teams call themselves 'Nads' so that they can say 'Go Nads!' It was funny when the first guy thought of it 25 years ago, but you know it's been overdone when you're in a league that includes the teams Nads 1, Nads 2 and Nads 3.

good as gold: everything's fine.

Often said when you've just fixed something. I always had niggling injuries as a footballer but I would always tell the club doctor that I was as good as gold, so that I could play, which would explain why I've had my hip replaced.

good one: what you say when someone says something funny.

Even if what they said wasn't funny, you can still say, 'Good one!' People say, 'Good one, Billy!' to me all the time, often when I haven't even opened my mouth, which is a bit of a worry.

good spread: a feast; when plenty of food has been put out on the table.

The CWA (Country Women's Association) are the best at putting on a good spread. Of course, it doesn't stay a good spread for too long once I turn up.

goolies: testicles.

It doesn't sound that serious when you say that you've been hit in the goolies, but trust me, it hurts just the same no matter what you call them.

goose: a bit of an idiot; a fool.

We've all been called a goose in our time. I got called a goose five times the other day, so I thought, *Bugger this, I'm leaving the house and going for a walk.*

Gr8: text for great.
Daggy now but it was cool when people first started texting.

grand final: what the Cats won in 2007 and 2009.
You bloody beauty!

granny flat: a self-contained flat in the backyard.
It's a very Aussie thing to have. It doesn't need to have a granny in it for it to be a granny flat, which is why I saw an ad for one the other day saying, 'For rent. Granny Flat. Granny not included.'

gross: disgusting
See fart jar (page 58). Or au naturel (page 12).

grubber: a ball that is bowled along the ground in a cricket match.
Made famous by Trevor Chappell's underarm delivery in that one-dayer against New Zealand. It must've been hard to be the younger brother of legends Ian and Greg, so you can't blame him for trying to get his own name up in lights. I didn't have a problem with his grubber. It was within the rules and it meant that we won. I remember watching it live and laughing at how upset people got. The only way it could've been any better was if we'd been playing the Poms.

**G-string: skimpy undies with a thin strip of
cloth that sits in your bum crack; also known as
'G-banger'.**
Chicks wear them a lot so they don't show panty lines. Some
guys wear them too. I'm not sure why. I couldn't think of
anything more uncomfortable than having undies wedged
between my butt cheeks. Well, I can think of stuff but that's
for another book.

**guts: determination; bravado; willingness to put your
body on the line.**
An important trait to have as a footballer, which makes it even
more surprising that I had a career. Then again, what I lacked
in guts, I made up for in charisma.

As a kid I always pronounced this as 'haich' when it is really supposed to be pronounced 'aich'. Sam Newman hates it whenever anyone pronounces it as 'haich', so we do it all the time just to give him the shits. I then tell him to get off his high horse. That's 'horse' spelt 'haich-O-R-S-E'. I've got too many other more important things to worry about in life than whether or not I pronounce 'H' properly. Anyway, I hate having my pronunciation corrected by other people. I'll speak however I like. It's my mouth and I'll use it whichever way I please. If that means stupid stuff comes out of it every now and again, then so be it. So, here's to the letter haich.

hack: a former great who is past their prime; someone who's old and worn out.

Fortunately, I retired before I became one . . . just. Also means how much you can put up with something. 'I couldn't hack training.' I may have been heard to say that on the odd occasion. To be fair, I did suffer most of my career with Osteitis Laziness.

hair of the dog: drinking alcohol the morning after.

It is supposed to be a good cure for a hangover. It makes sense. Your body is having withdrawal symptoms because you stopped drinking. Solution – start drinking again. Even if you don't have a hangover, just use it as an excuse to have a beer in the morning.

half-arsed, do it: to make a fairly weak attempt at something; to not give it your all.

Do that on the footy field at AFL level and it will be noticed. If the crowd misses it, then the TV replay will have captured it. It'll then be played over and over again in slow motion, and when they replay a half-hearted effort in slow motion it looks 100 times worse. I never backed into a pack half hearted. I was too busy on top of the pack, pulling down another speckie.

half-baked: an idea that wasn't thought through properly.

Like putting an AFL team in Western Sydney.

hammer: one of the best tools in the shed.

Bashing something with a hammer is good for the soul. Sometimes I'll put a nail in something for no other reason than it'll make me feel happy. The good thing about the hammer is that it keeps you honest. Any time you start getting cocky and over-confident with it, it'll whack you on the thumb. To hammer also means to give the opposition a beating in sport. Fortunately, in my day we gave out more hammerings than we got. In fact, our worst hammerings were dished out by Blighty on the training track.

hammered: drunk.
Really drunk. Just-capable-of-walking drunk. Been there.

hammy: hamstring.
You can do a hammy, pull a hammy, pull a hammy off the bone, twinge a hammy, strain a hammy, cork a hammy, or not do a hammy at all according to your coach, even though you've hobbled off the ground and it's obvious to everyone that you've done your hammy.

Hammy stretches were not like this in my day. I wish they were — this looks easy. But Blighty would never have allowed the smiling.

hand over fist: something done easily and rapidly.
Often refers to a business venture: 'They're making money hand over fist.' Certainly no business I've been associated with. Due to a lot of 'hand in the till', I'm tipping.

handcuffs: a device used to restrain someone who has been arrested, or for a more kinky purpose in the bedroom, which is why when I was arrested and sent home, I asked them to leave the cuffs on.
Didn't quite go to plan. I couldn't get my front-door key out and spent the night freezing me nuts off, huddled next to a tree in the garden.

hangover: the result of a big night out on the grog.
You know you have a hangover when the following symptoms

appear: a sore head, a dry mouth and the Darl vacuuming really loudly. She always happens to be vacuuming the morning after I've had a massive night. *The Hangover* is also a great movie. I fully recommend it. And also *Hangover Part II* – I reckon there will be quite a few of these movies at the rate we're going.

hanky: handkerchief.
A square piece of material used to blow your nose. Also used by magicians to do tricks. Hopefully not with the same one they used to blow their nose.

hanky panky: mucking around; being naughty.
Often refers to bedroom antics. In my case, hanky panky usually takes the form of me tripping over some shoes as I try to find the bed in the dark.

happy hour: an hour at a pub when the drinks are at discounted prices.
Often the sign at the pub says 'happy hour 6–8 p.m.' Yep, a two-hour happy hour. Not sure how that works but who's arguing? Some people like to make the most of this hour and drink all they can in the hope that it'll last them all night, which ends up turning the next hour into 'unhappy hour' for everyone else who has to put up with them.

hard hat: what blokes on building sites wear on their heads.
Everyone has to have one on because they're all convinced that a plastic yellow hat is going to protect them from a falling slab of concrete.

hard up: having little or no money.
Broke. Me the other day. I was playing Monopoly.

hat trick: when a bowler takes three wickets off three successive balls.

Doesn't happen very often and is quite exciting, especially during a slow test match when everyone is just about to doze off. I saw Warnie get a hat trick once. Three chicks with three successive text messages.

have a go: expression called out by a bloke who wants to fight another bloke.

An extended version of this is, 'Have a go, ya mug!' Blokes don't mind a punch-on and so an official invite like this is almost always accepted. The fight never starts straightaway. There is usually a bit of push and shove first. Never say, 'Have a go' to a bloke sitting in a chair because he could get up and be a lot taller than you thought. Never say, 'Have a go' while you're in a chair. It's very difficult to get a lot of power behind a punch while seated. Never say, 'Have a go' to the bloke in black with a number on him. He's the bouncer and has other mate bouncers ready to jump in. Never say, 'Have a go' to someone playing pool. He has a cue stick in his hand. Never say, 'Have a go' to that drunk bloke in the toilets. That bloke is you and you're looking in the mirror.

headbanger: a bloke who listens to heavy-metal music.

He likes to bang his head back and forth in time to the music. He then takes two Panadol and has a good lie down.

headstrong: the Darl.

In a good way, of course.

❀ health kick: a phase chicks go through where they focus on their health.

It usually involves a new exercise regime, a change of diet and the carrying around of a water bottle. They love to mention that they're on a health kick every chance they get, and you need to compliment them on how good they're looking every chance you get. It's also wise to stop mentioning what a waste of money that Ab King Pro was, and stop asking why it is on your side of the wardrobe. Guys don't go on a 'health kick', they 'work out'.

heart starter: a drink or meal you have early in the day to get you going.
It could be a coffee or a Red Bull.

 heart-throb: a bloke who chicks desire.
I think we all know who I'm talking about here. You were all thinking 'me', right?

hell for leather, going: doing something really fast.
When you're driving quickly to get somewhere on time, you often refer to it as going 'hell for leather'. One night I felt like I was in hell while dressed in leather, but I'm never going to one of those parties again.

Henry Ford: founder of the Ford Motor Company. Henry was instrumental in the development of the assembly line, which opened the door for mass production.

His Model T Ford is a classic and became the first affordable family car. Ford famously said that the customer could have a Model T Ford painted any colour they wanted, so long as it was black. He also sponsors the Cats, which is very generous of him. The relationship has been going on since 1925, which makes it the longest sports sponsorship in the world.

hens' night: chicks' version of a bucks' night.
Just a warning: never approach a bus load of chicks
on a hens' night – it is herd mentality out of control.
There's a chance you won't make it out alive. They're like a
plague of locusts; they devour everything in sight and leave
a hell of a mess for everyone else to clean up.

hide the sausage: euphemism for having sex.
Commonly heard in the expression, 'Let's play hide the sausage'. If you think you need to actually go out and buy some
sausages in order to play this game, you probably weren't listening very hard when you were given the 'birds and the bees'
talk.

highway robbery: being ripped off.
When you've paid too much for something or when a company charges over-the-top prices. Often applies to things
we don't have much choice about; for example, what we
pay for petrol or bank fees – that's highway robbery as
opposed to what you paid for this book, which is great value
for money.

hole in one: the ultimate golf shot.
You land the ball in the hole with your
tee shot. Many blokes go through their
whole life playing golf and never get
a hole in one, and I'm just rubbing it
in by reminding them about it. When
you do get a hole in one, it is tradition that you shout the bar, which
I did. The bar was packed, so I
bought a jug of beer and asked for
65 shot glasses.

Hollywood tape: the tape that chicks use to hold their dress to their boobs, so that their boobs don't pop out.

In big demand on Brownlow night. The Darl got really upset last year because I used all of her Hollywood tape when I was wrapping the Christmas presents.

homie: an abbreviated version of 'homeboy'; close friend.

What we blokes would call a mate. Can't wait to meet my homies for a beer soon.

honeymoon: the last time you and your wife had a good time.

honeymoon period: the first bit of any new situation where you can do no wrong.

Applies to new job, new missus. Usually lasts 3 months. Make the most of it.

Honkers: Hong Kong.

Great food and people, and good for haggling. In one of the markets there I haggled this guy down to $5 for this cool fig-urine. I was pretty happy with myself until I saw the same figurine in a two-dollar shop when I got back to Australia.

hoon: someone who drives fast and irresponsibly in a car.

I like doing donuts but only if they come in a box from Krispy Kreme.

hot spot: new technology used in cricket that shows where the ball has hit the bat.

I think it's called the 'hot spot' to make a pretty lame bit of technology sound really exciting.

hothead: someone who can't control their temper.
A hothead gets angry really quickly and then may do something stupid. I'm not a hothead. I've got no hair to keep the heat in my head.

household name: famous person.
Everybody knows who they are – Elvis, Robert De Niro, Kylie Minogue and Billy Brownless.

howzat?: what is yelled out when you're appealing in cricket.
If you think the batsman has got an edge or if it hit him in the pads directly in front or if it looks like he's been run out or if he's nowhere near being out but you just want to unsettle him, you yell, 'Howzat?!' If you're successful in your appeal, the umpire will put his finger straight up, or in Billy Bowden's case point it at someone in the crowd.

hunky dory: everything's okay; no need to worry.
When someone says this, that's the point I usually start getting suspicious.

hush money: money given to someone to keep their mouth shut.
What I give to my kids when I stuff up around the house so that they won't tell their mum. I must do it a fair bit because my son just bought a new flat screen for his bedroom.

'I think therefore I am' – the famous words uttered by philosopher René Descartes. What he was saying was that thinking about whether I exist proves that I actually exist. I stubbed my toe the other day and it really hurt. That was enough to prove to me that I exist. Anyway, 'I' is in the alphabet, so technically that means 'I' does exist. When you play sport, you are taught that 'I' isn't important. It's all about the team. When I was at Geelong, we were constantly being reminded that there is no 'I' in team, but there was a G. Ablett and he single-handedly made a hell of a difference. The letter I has really become popular thanks to all the gadgets made by Apple. There's the iPod, the iPhone and the iPad. If they could just invent the iWallet that makes its own iCash, we might be able to afford most of their stuff. Here are some more iWords.

I spy with my little eye: classic car-trip game.

Never took long to run out of things to spy, though. I still play it with my kids whenever we go on a long drive. Last year my son said, 'I spy with my little eye something beginning with "S".' By the time I'd worked out it was 'speed camera', there was a flash and it was too late.

Ian Fleming: author of the James Bond books.

He wrote twelve Bond novels and nine short stories. Not as commonly known is that he also wrote the children's story *Chitty Chitty Bang Bang*. It's true; I looked it up. Fleming actually worked in naval intelligence during the Second World War and so had plenty of experience to draw from when it came to writing his books. Thanks to him we have phrases like, 'Bond . . . James Bond' and 'Shaken not stirred' and 'How are ya, Cocko?' That last one is from the little-known Bond film *From Geelong with Love*.

Ice is a great cure-all for most kinds of injuries. If it hurts, put ice on it. Doesn't take long to feel better because you want to get warm. Use frozen peas as a substitute in a domestic situation.

ice: frozen water.

Plays a vital role in the keeping of beer cool. Comes in big bags that you need to smash on the ground to break up. A couple of things to think about before throwing the ice bag on the ground: 1) don't throw it so hard that the plastic bag breaks and the ice goes everywhere; 2) make sure your foot's out of the way.

ice: methamphetamine. A drug.

If you ask your kids to get some ice, just make sure it's clear that it's the sort that keeps your beer cool.

iceberg: a large mass of floating ice.

Responsible for the *Titanic*'s sinking, which also makes it responsible for the four hours of that bloody movie we had to sit through.

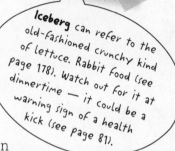

icebreaker: a line or joke that helps get a conversation or party started.

It makes people feel more relaxed so that they find it easier to talk to each other. I always find that saying, 'How's it going, Cocko?' usually does the trick. Here are some *not* so good icebreakers: 'What's that smell?', 'Anyone got a gun I can borrow?' and 'Out of my way, I think I'm going to vomit.'

Iceberg can refer to the old-fashioned crunchy kind of lettuce. Rabbit food (see page 178). Watch out for it at dinnertime — it could be a warning sign of a health kick (see page 81).

ice-cream headache: when you eat ice-cream too fast or sink your front teeth into it and a shot of pain is sent straight to your brain.

You are completely incapacitated for a minute, at which point, anyone could come up to you and steal your wallet or beat you up, and you would be unable to fight back. We all know the risks, but we continue to eat ice-cream because it is just so good.

ID: identification.

What you need to show when you go into a nightclub and then again seven hours later when you're at the police station.

identity crisis: a phase people go through where they experience self-doubt and aren't sure where they belong in this world.

If I ever feel that way, I just check my licence. Ah, yes, Billy Brownless. That's who I am.

idiocy: one of the many things I've mastered in my lifetime.

I'm not alone in this either. Some of my best friends are idiots.

if it is to be, it's up to me: a saying I like.

Just thought I'd put it in. A good thing to live by.

iffy: something that you're not sure about.

I'm usually a bit iffy about buying a hotdog from the bain-marie at the tenpin bowling alley. It always looks as if it's been sitting there for a couple of weeks. Still, that's nothing half a bottle of sauce won't fix.

I'll drink to that: a way of showing your support for someone else's opinion or idea.

It doesn't take a lot to get my support. 'It's twenty minutes past five.' I'll drink to that.

⭐ **ILY: I love you.**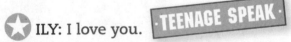

Another SMS acronym. Mainly used by girls. My daughter said 'ILY' to me once and I thought she meant she was a bit sicky.

in good nick: fit; a body in good condition.

In total, I was in good nick for about three weeks of my career.

in the mix: what a coach would say to you when there was no chance of you playing but he wanted to let you down gently.

You'd be in the mix with fifteen other blokes for one spot on the bench.

in-house: keeping things within a club or group.
If something has happened where a footballer has behaved badly or been involved in an embarrassing situation, the club will try and keep it in-house. This is a lot harder to do when the story appears on the front page of the paper and people all over the country are getting photos of you sent to their phone.

in-joke: a joke that only a certain group of people understand because they know information about its subject.
The in-joke could be at work, at home or at a footy club. I'd often walk in on the end of an in-joke. Everybody would be laughing and I'd ask what was so funny. To which they'd reply, 'Nothing.'

in-laws: your partner's parents.
Often referred to as 'the out-laws'. Let's face it, no man is ever going to be good enough for someone's daughter. It's okay to see them regularly, but it's still very important to keep a bit of distance between you and your in-laws. Never let them move in with you; this is just asking for trouble. Sometimes they will pop around unannounced, at which point you can hide behind the couch and pretend you're not home. Doesn't work as well when they've got a key.

inner-sanctum: deep inside a particular organisation; the select few who have access to the inner workings of an organisation.
I'd love to get into the inner-sanctum at Geelong. I keep knocking on the door but no one seems to want to answer.

innie: a bellybutton that goes in like a hole as opposed to an 'outie', which is a bellybutton that sticks out.

An innie is the more common and better-looking version but there are advantages to having an outie. You don't get bellybutton fluff. An innie can also refer to an inswinger in cricket. The bowler holds the ball a certain way so that it swings in to the batsman. If that's not working, you can always scratch the ball with a bottle cap.

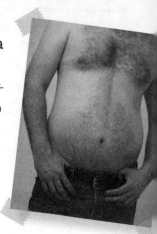

innings: the time that a team bats for in cricket.

Also refers to people's careers or lives. I intend to be around a lot longer and I hope I have a good innings, despite nearly running myself out a few times.

inside job: when a robbery has taken place with the assistance of someone who works for the company that was robbed.

Sometimes a robbery can go too smoothly and the police become suspicious straightaway that it was helped along by someone on the inside. It's like when one of your mates was working in the tuckshop at school. Having someone on the inside meant you were given more change back than you handed over in the first place.

insider trading: when someone who has some inside knowledge about stocks uses it to their advantage by selling or buying them.

It is a crime and if you get caught, it comes with a heavy penalty, usually involving jail time, which you may be able to avoid by paying off someone, using all the money you made on your insider trading.

IOU: a written note saying you owe someone money.
Not sure how legally binding it is. It probably just makes the lender feel better even though the borrower has no intention of paying back the dosh. I always pay my debts but, unfortunately, I keep forgetting who I've lent money to.

IQ: intelligence quotient.
Some sort of measurement as to how smart you are based on a test. Who'd want to do a test you didn't have to sit? I've never had my IQ measured and I don't plan to; you just end up with a number, and then they label you. Some people who think they're smart have come up with a way to tell everyone how smart they are. That's all it is, as far as I'm concerned. I reckon we are all clever in our own individual way. Some of us are street-smart, which is often the best way to be.

iron out: clean up with a bump or a punch.
Not seen as often in the AFL any more because the powers that be have outlawed most of the physicality. In the old days you would iron someone out and become a hero. I got ironed out once. What can I say, I wasn't scared of anyone. I was running one way while looking the other and before you knew it, BANG!, I'd been flattened. So, I bounced straight back up and started throwing a flurry of punches at the culprit. Don't know if you've ever seen a grown man throwing punches at a point post, but it was pretty embarrassing.

is the Pope Catholic?: the standard response whenever someone asks you a question they should know the answer to, like: 'Billy, do you want a beer?'

Or 'Billy, do you want another beer?' I wonder if the Pope ever uses it when he's asked a question. Question: 'Hey, Pope, are you looking forward to Easter?' Pope: 'Am I Catholic?!'

itchy feet: keen to do something or get involved.

When you're out injured and having to watch a game, you just can't wait to get back out there. I had a double dose of itchy feet once. I was out injured and had tinea as well.

it's me, not you: the break-up line you use to let your partner down easily.

You're putting the blame of the break-up solely on your own shoulders. In the end, it doesn't really make it any easier, especially since the 'it's me, not you' line has been exposed for what it really is – a poor attempt to end a relationship smoothly. Let's face it, breaking up is never easy and the only way to permanently cut ties with your partner is to fake your own disappearance. I tried it once but there's not much chance of a big bald bloke, yelling out 'Cocko!' all the time, being able to hide out anywhere.

it's your funeral: what's said to someone who has organised something that could go horribly wrong.

It often happens at work and you can always rely on your work buddies to get stuck into you about it. There is a place and a time for it, though. If your team is ten goals down going into the last quarter, I don't recommend saying to the coach, 'It's your funeral!'

I've seen a better head on a glass of beer: a way of describing someone you think is ugly.

A classic Aussie expression. Not sure why it is considered an insult. I think the head on a glass of beer looks beautiful.

One of my favourite sayings: Beauty is in the eye of the beer holder.

J is the best middle initial to have because it sounds so cool. Whether you're an AJ, a BJ, CJ, DJ, JJ, or even an MJ, you instantly have a cool nickname. Come to think of it, if your first initial is J, it sounds good as well – JA, JB, JD; they're all cool. God even gave his son cool initials – JC. Not to be confused with Jay-Z the rapper. He's got some great songs. I'd better get down to JB Hi-Fi and buy some.

jab: a short punch.

All I'm capable of throwing, with absolutely no power behind it at all, except, as I explained earlier, that one lucky time I got Gazza flush on the chin during boxing training. I suppose it's like that rule in prison. If you want everyone else's respect, you have to knock out the toughest guy there. There are other things that happen in prison that I won't go into here.

jack: a device used in changing a tyre on a car.

Anyone who is a jack of all trades knows how to use these. If I get a flat tyre I ask the Darl to ring the RACV. Enough said.

jack of: had enough of something.

I'm jack of mowing the lawn, so now I get a guy to do it. He's a lot better at it than me and doesn't spend an hour beforehand having a whinge about it. He's great. I've now got him taking the kids to training, washing my car and putting the bins out. I'm at the point now where I can just lie on the couch and watch the telly. The only thing I have to do is press the button on the remote to change the channel. I wonder how much he'd charge for that?

jack of all trades: someone who is good at a lot of things, especially when it comes to maintenance.

I'm not sure what the opposite of that is, but whatever it is, that's what I am.

jay walking

Jag: Jaguar car.

Also refers to when you pull something off that is considered difficult: 'I managed to jag it so that it was back on track.' There is also a fashion label called 'Jag', but they don't really cater for my style.

jam: something you spread on toast or scones.

You can also find it in a donut. Why are we always desperately looking for the jam in a hot donut, only to find that it burns the top of your mouth to the point that you can't even taste the rest of it? There are different types of jam. There's strawberry, raspberry, blueberry, apricot and, of course, there's toe jam. You know, that black stuff you find between your toes. I wouldn't recommend putting that on your toast. Jam also means to play musical instruments with others. Sometimes talented musicians can just play along together without having practised and still sound awesome. I would love to be able to jam with people. The last time I jammed was in a group of about thirty back in primary school and we were all playing the recorder. I'm pretty sure that didn't sound awesome.

James Bond: fictional character created by author Ian Fleming.

He's tough, he's cool, he gets all the ladies (reminding you of anyone else?), and all of his archenemies live in massive secret headquarters built inside old volcanoes. Who keeps selling old volcanoes to these guys? My favourite Bond is Sean Connery, and my favourite Bond movie is *Goldfinger*. To think, they actually named a Bond movie after a table-top-dancing bar in Melbourne.

jay walking: crossing the street as a pedestrian without using the lights.

I got booked for jay walking in the city once when I was in

99

a hurry and ran across the road to get to my car. The police nabbed me and I got a ticket. I told the officer I was running and so technically couldn't be booked for jay 'walking'. He crossed out the word 'walking' on the ticket and wrote 'running', and asked whether I was happier with that.

Jesse Owens: multiple Olympic gold medallist.

In 1936 in Berlin he won four track-and-field gold medals. Hitler was the leader of Germany at the time and he desperately wanted the Olympics to be a showcase of the supremacy of the German Aryan race. He was not too impressed when Jesse Owens, an African American, put that notion to bed with victories in the 100m, 200m, broad jump and 4 x 100-metre relay.

jiffy: a short amount of time.

Often used by people who need to pop out and then come back. 'I'll be back in a jiffy.' A jiffy could be anything from one to twenty minutes. Half an hour is probably too long to be a jiffy. If it was, then we wouldn't play four quarters in a game, we'd play four jiffies. On the other hand, half-time nearly qualifies as a jiffy. Jiffy time sounds like so much more fun that half-time, especially during a grand final when you could have 'jiffy time entertainment'.

Jimmy Bartel: Geelong superstar and Brownlow medallist.

Quietly spoken and unassuming but tough as nails on the football field. Very, very good-looking man, who has in the past struggled to find a date for the Brownlow, which is a surprise because 1) as mentioned, he is a very attractive man; and 2) there is no shortage of ladies who would sell their own grandmother to go to the Brownlow. I think he's okay now, though – not that I want to go into it in too much detail here. Put it this way, somebody finally asked him out.

jockey: little bloke who rides horses in races.

When I was young I wanted to be a jockey. It looks like a really exciting profession. Unfortunately, I grew too big, and unless horses start growing bigger, I've got no chance. As a punter, I have my favourite jockeys. I may bet on them because they have ridden a previous winner of mine, or I like the way they ride, or I've simply got no idea about the horse's form. It's important to remember that without jockeys there'd be no Melbourne Cup. We need the horses as well but, then again, 24 jockeys running around the track would be pretty funny.

jocks: undies.

They come in different colours and pat- terns but all do the same thing. We blokes only replace them as they literally fall apart. One hole is never a problem. Two holes is a bit annoying but bearable. When the holes become so big that you don't need to take off your jocks to go to the toilet, it's a sign you might want to buy some new ones.

jockstrap: sports underwear designed to support a man's private parts.

When you run or jump, certain parts of your body bounce around with you. A jockstrap helps keep that to a minimum by providing solid support for your genitals. Most blokes are just happy wearing their normal everyday jocks for sport, which makes it more interesting when a player gets dacked in a game on the telly. You do get to see a bizarre range of colours and designs, but then you also get kids hassling their mums with, 'I want bright-green jocks like Alan Didak!'

Joe Blow: a made-up bloke we use when we're trying to explain stuff.

He represents the average man. Let's hope Joe Blow buys this book, hey.

jog: the fastest speed I am capable of running.

A sprint for me is jogging while bobbing my head up and down at the same time. A lot of people jog to keep fit but some experts say walking is better for you than jogging. I'm waiting to hear that sitting on the couch is even better than walking, then I'll be set.

jollies: getting excited by doing something.

We all get our jollies for different reasons. I get my jollies hearing the 'pʊssst' sound of a stubby being opened.

joshing: joking; kidding.

You can have fun with a mate by telling him some devastating news that you've made up and just as he's about to cry, you say, 'Only joshing.' At which point you need to be on your guard because he'll be likely to throw a punch.

joy-ride: a crazy ride in a car.

Often refers to driving around in a stolen car. Doesn't apply to family holiday car trips. No joy there.

jug: the biggest receptacle you can buy beer in at a pub.

It's usually always cheaper to buy it in this form. When you do buy a jug, the person behind the bar always asks, 'How many glasses would you like?' To which I always respond, 'Just a straw, thanks.'

jugs: boobs.

jumbuck: a sheep.

For those who have always wondered what they were singing about in 'Waltzing Matilda'. It's important to know. Often we just get caught up in the music and don't think about what the lyrics mean. I lost track of the number of times in the early '90s when I'd hear middle-aged women on the streets singing to themselves, 'When I think about you I touch myself.'

jump the queue: what rude people do to avoid having to stand in a line or wait their turn.

At the end of the day it doesn't matter who you are, you shouldn't expect any special treatment. I don't care if you're Joe Blow or a former AFL superstar and popular personality like me, we're all equal. My favourite waiting-in-line experience is when you go to the doctors. It doesn't matter what time your appointment was, you need to add twenty minutes.

There are always heaps of people waiting and I love looking at everyone because some of them actually think that by sitting there and looking really sick, it might help them jump the queue.

Jumper leads are in a similar category to jacks (see page 98). Some people can always get cars going. It's a good idea to make sure some of those people are your friends.

jumper leads: leads that connect the batteries of two cars to help start the one with a flat battery.

Most of us at some stage in our lives have been asked the following question: 'You wouldn't happen to have any jumper leads, would ya?' What they actually mean is,

'Could you tow me to the mechanic – thanks.' Oh, and there's the time the bouncer on the door at the nightclub put jumper leads round my neck and said, 'Now don't start anything, will you?' (Dad joke, see page 38.)

junior: a kid; Gary Ablett; a bloke's son.

If the son is named after the dad, then 'junior' is often added to their name, or that's just what everyone calls them anyway. I use it a lot when I forget a mate's kid's name. When I'm having a really bad day, I'll use it when I forget my own son's name: 'Hey, Junior, get in here!'

junk: stuff blokes have to get rid of.

Often involves a trailer and trip to the tip if you've missed the hard rubbish collection. There's a good saying that one man's trash is another man's treasure but here's a handy bit of advice: the missus will usually think whatever you've found on the street is definitely junk. Also note: nothing she buys is ever junk.

junk food: really, really tasty food.

Sure, not considered by the experts to be good for you, but it sure feels good eating it. Maybe it's just me. I can't help myself. It must be an in-built thing. When I met with my careers counsellor in Year 10, 'nutritionist' wasn't one of the occupations that came up as an option for me. As they say, as long as you eat junk food in moderation, you'll be okay. I really hope that three dim sims a day comes under the moderation guidelines.

junk time: the bit at the end of the game when the players waste time because the result cannot change.

We've borrowed this from American sports – they also call it 'garbage time'. You know it's happening when the players kick the ball short distances backwards to rack up each other's possessions and the crowd starts booing. Or they start cheering because of their dream team points.

just not on: getting angry about something that happened or someone did.

Like a pub shutting its doors before official closing time – that's just not on. Then the bouncer throwing you out because you're arguing about the closing time – that's just not on. Then having a cab driver refuse to take you home because you're too pissed – that's just not on. You eventually find your way home, crawl into bed and snuggle up to the Darl for a bit of kissy-kissy, and she says to you, 'That's just not on.'

'KFC' is my favourite K word. It's short for Kentucky Fried Chicken. They abbreviated it so as not to put people off with the word 'fried'. Wouldn't bother me, I can tell you. In fact, if the word 'fried' was still used in the name, I reckon I'd be even more tempted to go there. I also shop a lot at KMart. Not sure what the 'K' in KMart stands for, but I hope it's for something funny, like Keith. A 'k' is a kilometre. Whenever we trained, I'd always laugh when a teammate asked me how many ks I'd run. Ks? Like it was going to be more than one. Special K is a very popular brand of breakfast cereal. It contains 12 per cent of your recommended total daily intake of protein. Okay, so I'm reading off the packet. You've got me. I wonder if K-Rudd will have a crack at reading this book . . . on second thoughts, maybe it's not for him. More K words coming right up.

kamikaze: someone who dives in head-first without fear; used to describe a dangerous act.

The Japanese kamikaze pilots in the Second World War would fill their planes with bombs and fly directly into the Allied forces' ships. That's why it was very important for the ships to shoot these planes out of the sky beforehand. Fortunately, the Allies won the battle of the Pacific, and we will never forget the heroism of those who fought for us.

kangaroo: native Australian marsupial; national symbol of Australia.

Beloved creature that looks cute and cuddly until you get up close to a big one, which, if provoked, could knock your head off with a couple of kicks. Kangaroo meat is available in heaps of restaurants but I still can't bring myself to eat it. I don't want it to take off. Before you know it, we'll have wombat soup and koala satays.

Kangaroos: North Melbourne, Australian Rules football club.

My mate James 'JB' Brayshaw is the president of North Melbourne and doing a great job, unless, of course, by the time this is published he's no longer there, in which case, I say he had it coming and deserved to get the arse.

kaput: broken; stuffed; doesn't work any more.

My lawnmower is kaput. What a shame. Really should get that fixed one day. I reckon they should use 'kaput' more. When the ATM isn't working, instead of the sign saying, 'This machine is temporarily unavailable,' it should get right to the point: 'This machine is kaput!'

keeper: wicketkeeper; the bloke who stands behind the wicket in cricket.

Sometimes shortened to 'wicky'. In backyard cricket you can also have an automatic keeper. Any time a batsman snicks the ball, they're out. As good as they are at never dropping a catch, the automatic keeper has a pretty poor record when it comes to stumpings.

keg: barrel full of beer.

Most kegs hold 50 litres and are made of stainless steel. Kegs are pressurised. A lot of blokes get a keg for their party but have trouble tapping it and the beer doesn't come out properly. What started as a truly great party idea easily turns into a disaster. Kegs are also very heavy, so be careful moving them around. Heaps of blokes wake up after a keg party with a hangover and four broken toes, wondering what happened.

kelpie: Australian sheep dog.

Great working dog that can muster livestock with very little guidance or instruction. I'm thinking of getting one for around the house to help keep the kids in line.

kick in: to make a contribution.

If you're with a group of people and someone suggests buying a pizza, then everyone 'kicks in' some cash. Always be wary of the person who 'doesn't feel like pizza' and doesn't kick in: when the pizza arrives they often manage to snare a piece anyway. I don't know if it's just me, but tightarses really get under my skin. I'm not talking about people who are trying to save money and careful with what they spend. I'm talking about people in a group situation who are happy for others to pay more even though they've pretty much enjoyed the same meal. Then again, tightarses will always exist. We all know one and will continue to go out with them, even though we know what they're like. One of them might be reading this book right now, having borrowed it from a friend because they were too tight to pay for a copy themselves.

kick on: to party on; to keep going even though most people have headed home.

After a day at the races, especially during the Spring Carnival, everyone is usually keen to kick on. That is until they get to the exit gate at Flemington and realise that they haven't organised how they are going to get out of there. They start walking, with no real plan, hoping to get a cab somewhere. Pretty soon the momentum is gone, everyone is tired, their feet are sore, the alcohol is starting to wear off, and that's when the arguing begins. Eventually, you arrive at Crown Casino and are so knackered that you find a corner to prop yourself up in, and then spend the rest of the night trying not to fall asleep. The funny thing is, the next year at the Spring Carnival someone suggests kicking on and you go, 'Yeah, I'll be in that!'

kick the habit: to give up a bad habit that you have.

It could be smoking, drinking or drug-taking. Luckily, I don't smoke and have never taken drugs. My drinking makes up for them anyway. I tried to give up the grog once. I went on the patches. I took the VB labels off the stubbies and stuck them on my arms.

killing time: finding something to do while you are waiting.

Often you'd have heaps of time sitting in the rooms before a game of footy. Each player had their own way of using that time to prepare for the game. Some players listened to music, others would sit in the corner and basically meditate and some would read the footy *Record*. I used to like seeing how much stuff I could stick in Buddha Hocking's head of thick, tight curly hair. Once I got three footy boots in there without any of them falling out. Yeah, in hindsight, I probably could have used that time to focus on the game ahead a bit more.

King Dick: someone who thinks they are better than everyone else.

A person who behaves in such a way that everyone around them is made to feel inferior, which usually prompts one of them to say, 'He thinks he's King Dick!' If you become King Dick, I'm not sure if your wife automatically becomes Queen Dick.

king hit: a big punch that knocks someone senseless.

The person being hit usually doesn't see it coming. The worst kind of king hit is a 'king hit behind play'. This often results in a serious injury, and has seen footy players suspended for long periods. The AFL has clamped down on violence and the king hit is virtually extinct, which is sad for those players who, in the past, were drafted purely on their ability to deliver a king hit.

kitchen tea: an all-female party thrown for the bride-to-be by her friends and family.

Everyone brings a gift and they play a few games. I think that's what goes on. The Darl only ever gives me snippets of information, and I don't want to sound too keen to find out more about what goes on. For all I know, they could've been playing nude Twister with a visiting Russian dance troupe. Come to think of it, I thought I could smell vodka!

Kiwi: a New Zealander.

I love listening to them speak. New Zulunders have a viry destunctuv eggsint.

knackerated: when you land testicles-first on something after a fall.

Skateboarders do it a lot: they skate down a handrail, lose the board and then hit the rail balls first. Testicles aren't very good at handling being squashed against a railing under the full force of a large male body travelling at speed. The pain is horrendous, and winning the major prize on *Funniest Home Videos* doesn't make the pain go away.

knackers: testicles.

Also a friendly name you'd call another bloke: 'G'day, knackers!' A term of endearment from one bloke to another.

knob: an idiot.

Someone who puts everyone else offside. A knob is like a dickhead but worse. It is possible to start as a dickhead and work your way up to being a knob. A tough career path but if you follow your dreams, you just never know.

knock shop: a brothel.

Often identified by a red light out the front, which I think gives it a bit of a negative vibe. They should have a green light out the front, so that it's all go, go, go!

knockabout: a likeable bloke who's a bit rough around the edges and doesn't necessarily follow the rules.

I've been called a knockabout sort of bloke before and I take that as a compliment. Then again, if someone says to me, 'You're not as fat in person as I thought you were,' I take that as a compliment as well. I can't be too picky.

knock-off: a cheap imitation of the genuine product.

Aussie holiday-makers often return from Bali with a suitcase full of knock-offs. In some cases, the name of the product wouldn't even be spelt correctly. It mightn't work any more, but I still reckon my Rolax watch looks pretty good.

knockout: a hot-looking chick.

Very complimentary to a woman. 'Wow, she's a knockout!' And if you say that in front of her boyfriend, you may end up being knocked out.

knot: the result of tying rope.

Blokes find knots very handy, especially when they're taking a trailer load of stuff to the tip or picking up something big that sticks out of the boot, like a new TV. A good strong secure knot is what is required there. The one you use to tie your shoelaces just won't cut it, I'm afraid. Many a hard day's work has come undone because of a poorly tied knot. The worst thing about a drive to the tip is dodging all the rubbish flying off the back of the trailer belonging to the bloke in front of you because he hasn't tied the load down properly. If you don't know how to tie a knot, look it up on the net. Some blokes are lucky. They've been to Scouts and know every knot there is. I can't believe in all my years at Scouts I didn't learn how to tie a knot, but yet I'm great at baking brownies. Hang on . . . I think I may have been in the wrong group.

Tying the **knot** means getting married, something I am a big fan of. I mean, weddings are great! Lots of free beer, lots of mates . . . what more could a bloke want?

'L' is what you have on the back and front of your car when you're learning to drive. It's so that other drivers can see that you're a learner and drive right up your bum, before overtaking and then cutting you off. It's not much fun being a learner driver. It's very difficult to look cool with the L-plates on and your mum sitting next to you. The car may as well have big training wheels sticking out the side. You're certainly not pulling up at the lights, winding down your window and trying to chat up the hot chick in the car next to you. 'L' is also the symbol people hold to their forehead, using their finger and thumb, as a way of telling someone that they're a loser. It's probably been done to death now but that move was big there for a while. Just make sure you use your right hand and not your left, otherwise the 'L' is back to front and you've called yourself a loser.

lab rat: a species of rat bred for scientific purposes.
They are used for research in medicine and other fields. Scientific research on rats has led to advances in medicine that have helped humans. Probably doesn't make the rats feel any better, though.

ladder: a thing you climb up.
It assists tradesmen in their jobs, as well as home handymen. Every bloke has to have a ladder and no one gets as excited as a bloke who, after carefully surveying a job, says to his wife, 'I'd better get the ladder.' Yeah, that shows you mean business! Unfortunately, it's what you do at the top of the ladder that really counts. It's not until you get up there that you realise how hard it is to hold a bracket and a drill, all while trying to balance yourself and defy gravity. Even the most skilled high-trapeze artists use a net.

ladies' man: a bloke who chases and gets the ladies.
It's a bit of an art form and the skills are passed down from generation to generation. I won't go through it in this book, in case some chicks read it and ruin it for us all.

If you think you're a bit of a **ladies' man**, check creep (page 33), dickhead (page 39), knob (page 112) and tool (page 218) just to make sure.

lager: a beer.
It differs from other beers due to the type of yeast used and the way it is fermented. I'm not an expert on the process of making it but I am in the process after that, which involves me paying for it over the bar, the barman pouring it into a glass and then me tipping it down my throat . . . over and over again.

lagerphone: a musical instrument made from bottle tops nailed to a stick.

You use another stick to bang the stick with the bottle tops on it. I've been involved in the making of lots of lagerphones. I drink the beer they get all the bottle tops from. INXS have devoted so much energy to trying to find a replacement singer when maybe all they needed was to add a lagerphone to the band.

lairise: to show off, especially on a football field.

I was often pulled up for lairising by the coach. I said to him, 'I don't just talk the talk, I walk the walk.' He said, 'Well, how about you run the run and try to keep up with your opponent.'

lamington: an iconic Aussie cake.

Square in shape, made from a sponge cake and covered in chocolate icing and coconut. A dinky-di proper one has jam in the middle. Whenever I eat one without jam, I feel completely ripped off. The origin of the lamington is up for debate as there are different theories floating around. Queensland's governor at the turn of the twentieth century was Lord Lamington, and one story goes that he had guests around and his chef had to quickly give them something to eat, so he improvised with an old sponge cake. The guests loved it so much they asked for the recipe. Just think, if the pizza shop had been open, lamingtons may never have been invented.

lap dance: a stripper's dance where the bloke is sitting on a chair and the dancer is in contact with him or very close to him.

Different states of Australia have different rules as to how close the stripper can get. Have I ever had a lap dance, you ask? Once, and it wasn't a great experience. It was Barry Stoneham in the rooms after a game. Thought I would've got more for my $20, to be honest.

laughing all the way to the bank: said of someone who has made a lot of money.

They've got so much cash that they're laughing as they deposit it at the bank. They're also probably crying as they leave after discovering how much they'll be paying in fees.

lay an egg: to fail at something; stuff it up.

It could be in relation to something you've made or an event you've organised: 'I think you've laid a massive egg with this one.' I've laid heaps of eggs at my place in my attempts at being a handyman.

lay into someone: to beat someone up.

Also means to verbally abuse someone. You can do both to someone if you want to make sure you've got the definition covered.

lead foot: someone who drives too fast.

You don't see as many these days. This may have something to do with speed cameras being at every intersection. Sure, they've made the road a bit safer but they've also taken the fun out of speeding up and trying to sneak through an amber light before it turns red.

Car For Sale

lemon: a car that doesn't work or that keeps breaking down.

A car needs to be reliable (like my Ford) and there's nothing worse than driving around thinking that your car could stop anywhere, anytime. It's difficult to sell a lemon. You

don't want to rip someone else off and burden them with it. That's where the cliff comes into it . . .

lie low: to hide away from everyone.

A lot of your criminal types will be lying low so that the police or their enemies can't find them. I'd always lie low if I'd played a bad game. After some games I'd have to wear a fake beard and sunglasses.

light years: a long time.

When they talk about distance in space they use light years. One of those light years is about 10 trillion kilometres. And I thought the drive from Geelong to Melbourne was a long way.

You can get deluxe model **Li-los** with velour tops now, like the one I have on stand-by for when I get home hammered (see page 79). Trouble is, it's really hard to use the foot pump in that condition.

li-lo: an inflatable mattress.

The most versatile of beds. When you went on summer holidays, you could sleep on it at night and take it to the beach during the day. The fun didn't stop there. At night you'd wait for your brother to fall asleep, and then you'd pull out his li-lo plug so that it would slowly deflate and he'd wake up on the hard floor.

lingo: language; a way of speaking.

Some things have their own lingo. Some people don't understand computer lingo, and a lot of people don't understand Billy lingo. I say, 'Listen harder, Cockos!'

Lionel Rose: first Aborigine to win a world title in boxing.

Grew up in Jacksons Track in Victoria and was taught to box by his father, Roy. From humble beginnings he went on to become bantamweight champion of the world when he defeated Fighting Harada in 1968. He defended his title a number of times and even embarked on a singing career in the '70s, which included the hits songs 'I Thank You' and 'Please Remember Me'. That's pretty impressive. There aren't a lot of boxer/singers out there. Although, I do hear the Gallagher brothers from Oasis can get a bit punchy when they're not happy.

Lions: Brisbane, AFL football team.

Originally the Fitzroy Lions. People are still hurt by that. Football runs deep in people's veins. You disband a team (call it a relocation, if you like) and you rip the hearts out of die-hard supporters. Nothing I can say here can ever fix that but at the very least I can acknowledge it. I was fortunate enough to play against Fitzroy and some of their champions. It was a sad day when the AFL world said goodbye to Fitzroy in 1996. For their last ever game they played Fremantle at Subiaco. Old verses new, I suppose. It really represented where the future of football was heading in this country.

liquid lunch: beer or other alcohol for lunch.

People spend too much time trying to decide what to eat for lunch each day. Do I get something hot? I can't have that, I had it yesterday. Do I get a salad? Is there onion in that? Maybe I should go vegetarian? Have a liquid lunch instead and you won't have to worry about all that stuff . . . and yes, beer is vegetarian.

little beauty: a cry of joy over something good that has happened.

Heard many a time in the TAB when someone's horse flies home to win: 'You little beauty!' It is usually accompanied by the sounds of the other punters ripping up their tickets and cursing their horses in, how can I put this, a very unsavoury manner.

little boys: cocktail frankfurts.

Kids love 'em – I usually prefer a hot dog.

lob: to turn up; an unexpected arrival.

Relatives are notorious for lobbing up and making themselves comfortable. Within a couple of hours they've cleaned out the fridge and the pantry. As well as a '<u>No</u> Hawkers' sign on my front door, I might get a '<u>No</u> Lobbers' one. By the way, the '<u>No</u> Hawkers' sign refers to people who are trying to sell me stuff and all Hawthorn supporters.

local: the closest pub to your place.

It really is your local if the barman recognises you on sight or knows your name. Some people may have a few pubs close by, so your local would be the one you prefer to go to most. I'm not that picky. I even have a local when I go on holidays somewhere.

local rag: the local newspaper.

Usually filled with more ads than news stories. The big story on the front cover may involve any of the following: an old lady, a cat, a kindergarten, a local theatre group, a tree, a creek, a busy intersection, or someone winning an award. I'm pretty sure I read a story once that somehow included everything I've just mentioned. Geelong's local rag, the *Geelong Advertiser*, wanted to honour Gary Ablett, so it changed its name one week to the *Geelong Ablettiser* and all the pages were blue. Thankfully, they weren't honouring James Podsiadly because the *Geelong Podsiadvertiser* is a bit of a mouthful.

LOL: laugh out loud, in text talk
You have to be careful with this one – it used to mean 'lots of love'. So if you get a text from a mate saying their dog just died, it's not appropriate to reply 'LOL'.

lolly water: flavoured soft drink.
A term used when getting stuck into one of your mates when he isn't drinking beer: 'Are you on the lolly water again?' Besides, it pretty much is a lolly in a bottle. It's full of colour and sugar. Not what a bloke wants to be drinking when he's out. He may as well have stayed at home.

❀ love: a very important word
When you first hear it from your girlfriend, be very careful how you respond. Don't say I didn't warn you.

low-life: not a very nice bloke; a scumbag; someone who behaves in a disgraceful or offensive way.
One of the worst things you can call someone. I don't consider myself a low-life but heaps of opposition supporters used to call me that when I was playing. I remember most of your faces, so I expect an apology if I see you walking down the street.

lump in the throat: to get emotional.
In the last quarter of the 2007 Grand Final when the Cats were
on the verge of breaking that premiership drought, I had a
lump in my throat the size of a donut. Hang on, I think that
actually was a donut stuck in my throat. I've really got to learn
to chew those things properly.

M is James Bond's boss. It'd be so much easier just having one letter as your name. It wouldn't take long to sign anything and people wouldn't have any trouble spelling it. Football commentators would be able to pronounce it and supporters wouldn't struggle to yell it out when you did something spectacular. Your team-mates couldn't come up with a stupid nickname because they'd have nothing to work with. It'd just be M. There'd always be 'Big M', I suppose, but that'd be about it. Okay, they could also call you 'Golden Arches', as in the yellow M on top of the Macca's stores. If they put their heads together, they could maybe have even come up with the nickname 'MT', as in empty. Come to think of it, there are heaps of stupid nicknames they could give you. So, there you have it. It doesn't matter how small and uncomplicated your name is, people will always be able to make fun of it. What about M&Ms? I could do this all day!

macaroni and cheese: the meal you'd always get on a school camp and now refuse to eat as an adult.

The worst thing about having crap food on camp was dishes duty. You'd get a second and much longer whiff of the same meal but this time colder and stuck to a plate. Like everyone else, I always thought camp food was crap. That was until I tried cooking.

mad as a cut snake: crazy; completely unbalanced.

Blighty. I love him, don't get me wrong, but he's off his rocker.

madam: a woman running a brothel.

Quite a formal title for someone in that job. I played professional sport at an elite level and the best title bestowed on me was 'boofhead'.

mag: a magazine.

Something you read at the doctors or dentists while you are waiting. Always an interesting experience. When you get there, you are determined not to read one of the trashy mags on the table but then after having waited twenty minutes, you give in and pick one up, only to fall into its trance. *Wow!* you think to yourself when you read that Tiger Woods has been sleeping around with heaps of women again, only to realise that the magazine is a year old and the story you're reading is about his original series of indiscretions. Hey, doctors! You're making a fortune, go and buy some new magazines instead of going through people's recycling bins.

Magpies: Collingwood Football Club, the biggest AFL club in Australia.

A juggernaut. Not sure who the president is. He likes to stay out of the limelight.

mags: wheels.
Good wheels maketh the car, I say. There are so many types of mag wheels you can buy. These days you really are spoilt for choice. Most cars you buy have a range of mags to suit that particular model. They look great too. They're chrome, they're shiny and they look pretty special. Unfortunately, it's only a matter of time before the mag meets its archenemy – the gutter. Concrete and chrome just don't mix. The first mark on your mags really hurts, but the second mark hurts a lot less and then you can drive around without worrying about getting the first mark. Anyway, I know a guy who can buff out those marks for about $50. I don't really know a guy, but that's what everyone says to me.

make tracks: to leave.
When it's time to go, you'll often say to the hosts that you have to make tracks. In other words, you just want to get the hell out of there.

man crush: a bloke admiring another bloke purely based on his great blokeness and nothing else.
Many blokes have man crushes on footballers like Jonathan Brown and Luke Hodge. They're both a real man's man. Tough as, and good blokes.

man in white: umpire.
These days, though, they're in all sorts of colours. You'll see them in green, red, orange and yellow. I'm surprised they haven't been sued by The Wiggles for trying to cash in on their success.

manual: a car with gears.

Any bloke who can only drive an automatic needs to take a good hard look at himself. I refuse to get in a shout with a bloke before I've seen him take off in a manual on a hill without the assistance of the handbrake.

marching orders: when someone is told to leave.

They could've been given the sack at work or told they're no longer required at a football club or even told by their missus to go and find somewhere else to live.

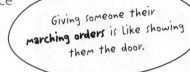

Giving someone their *marching orders* is like showing them the door.

marked man: a bloke who's become a target after having done something that put him in a bad light.

If you're playing footy and you've whacked someone in the first quarter, you are a marked man for the rest of the game and the next few you play against that team. There's nothing worse than being a marked man because you don't know when you're going to cop it back. I'm still on edge and looking over my shoulder every time I walk down the street because of stuff I did on the footy field fifteen years ago.

mascara: eye make-up; used to darken, colour and thicken the eyelashes.

When chicks cry, the mascara is the stuff that runs down their face. That's when they always say, 'Is my mascara running?' and you reply, 'No, it's fine.' That's all great until you get home, they find a mirror and realise they've been looking like Alice Cooper all night.

mash: mashed potatoes.
When I was a kid it was considered one of the plainest dishes but now for some reason it's become a delicacy in a lot of restaurants. It's weird now to go out and pay good money for a steak on a bed of mash. A bed of mash? I'll only ever see it as a scoop or a clump of mash.

massage parlour: a place you go for a massage but is also believed to give you a bit more.
Often the front for a brothel. The only way to know for sure is to go and find out for yourself. All in the name of research, of course.

mate: a bloke's friend, one of his best buddies.
Although, 'mate' can still be used when referring to people you've just met or even complete strangers: 'Hey, mate. How much for this flat screen TV?' It can even be used in anger: 'Hey, mate! What do you think you're doing?' It's one of the most iconic Australian words we have. Americans trying to do an Aussie accent will always throw the word 'mate' in there. A collective group of friends are called your mates. They could be your schoolmates, workmates or footy mates. I've got mates I have met through other mates. So, that makes them mates of mates. You can say it quickly – 'mate'. You can draw it out to 'ma-a-a-ate!' When excited you can draw it out even further to 'ma-a-ha-ha-ate!' What a great word! And it belongs to us!

mates' rates: the payment scale used when you do a job for a mate or vice versa.
It could be half as much as you would normally pay. That's why it's important to have one mate who's a carpenter, one

who's an electrician, one who's a plumber and one who's an accountant (to make sure the mates' rates actually do work out to be cheaper).

MCG: Melbourne Cricket Ground.
Affectionately known as 'The G'. Australian landmark. One of the greatest experiences of my life was standing out in the middle of that stadium in front of 90 000 fans there to watch me play. I'm sure there were a couple of people who came to see Gary Ablett play as well.

meat market: a bar or nightclub you can go to where it is easy to pick up.
These days, dating websites seem to have that covered.

mental blank: a brain freeze.
You have trouble remembering stuff. You can't think of anything. Happens to me regularly. The harder I try to think of something the worse it gets. It's like my brain knows I'm putting pressure on it and refuses to come to the party. It's not even responding to me trying to think of more to write or this bit. Let me bang my head with my hand . . . nah, still got nothing.

Merc: Mercedes Benz.
I wonder if Schapelle Corby's sister, Mercedes, is called Merc for short?

Mickey Mouse: rhyming slang for grouse.
Something that is excellent. It can, however, also refer to something that

is childish and basic. Mmm ... interesting. Mickey Mouse can either mean a very good thing or a very bad thing. How would you know which way it is being used? I just got a mental image of poor Mickey being pulled in opposite directions and crying out for help in that ridiculous high-pitched voice of his. Just when are his balls going to drop?

miffed: upset; annoyed; not angry enough to do something about it.

I get miffed when I buy a burger and the slice of tomato they've put in there is the end bit. It's the least tasty part and has got more skin on it than any other bit. I get miffed about that but never enough to go and ask for another one. If it happened twice in a row at the same place, it'd be a different story, though. It'd be on between me and the fifteen-year-old kid behind the counter, and he'd bear the full brunt of my miffiness.

mile-high club: the club you automatically join when you have sex on a plane while it is in the air.

Not an easy thing to do. The toilet is the only place you could get away with it, and I hate going in there to go to the toilet, let alone anything else. Every time I go into one, some bloke has just come out waving the newspaper in front of his face. I can't imagine anything romantic happening in there. The best place would be the cockpit. It's got a great view as well. You'd just have to rely on the pilot to keep his eyes shut.

MILF: hot mum; yummy mummy.

The letters in MILF stand for 'Mother I'd Like to Flirt with', I think ... but I could be wrong.

missus: wife.

Only used when talking to other blokes. Never used in front of your wife because it wouldn't go down too well. Feel free to try, though, and see how it goes.

⭐ **mint: really good.**

If something is awesomely great, it's 'mint'. So, I'm guessing that this book is 'mint'.

mo: moustache.

Has made a bit of a comeback, especially during Movember. A great idea that raises money and awareness for men's health. I reckon it's a fantastic cause and a fun time of the year for all. I'd grow a mo but it would take me about three months.

money tree: something wives think grows out the back with $100 notes on it.

They must think money grows on trees, otherwise why do they keep asking for so much of it?

monkey suit: a dinner suit; black tie.

Compulsory attire for the Brownlow medal. The AFL cracked down on the dress code a few years ago, yet they let Freo wear red, green and purple jumpers.

moron: an idiot; a person who says or does something stupid.

There are a few out there, I can tell you. The government should pass a law to have all morons' foreheads stamped with the letter 'M' so that the rest of us can see them coming and take whatever action we need to avoid them.

mug shot: a photo taken when you're arrested.

Never very flattering. I've never had a mug shot taken but I can't imagine I could look any worse than I do in my licence or passport photo. At least when I get pulled over, I can put the cops in a good mood by handing over my licence. By the time they've stopped laughing at my photo, they've forgotten what they pulled me over for.

Mug shots are never flattering. This photo could also be used for hard hat (see page 80) and tool (see page 218).

'N' is often used in place of the word 'and' like in fish 'n' chips, or Wet'n'Wild theme park on the Gold Coast, or Bras 'n' Things. Not sure why I thought of Bras 'n' Things. It just came to me. Maybe I shopped there in a previous life. Musical groups like to use 'n' as well. There's Salt-n-Pepa, Bliss N Eso, and even 'N Sync, but give me a bit of rock 'n' roll any day.

nab: National Australia Bank.

They ran a big advertising campaign announcing they'd split up with the other banks. Just how many of them were together in the first place? What sort of finance-fuelled bank orgy were they all involved in? I don't think we'll ever know but like every relationship break-up, it can only get uglier. Nab also means to capture someone. 'I nabbed a bloke trying to steal my garden hose.' That's just an example, by the way. I never nabbed a guy stealing my garden hose. I don't even know if I've got a garden hose. Yep, obviously been a while since I've ventured out there.

nag: a horse that is no good.

One that has usually cost me money. Nag also means to continually pester or harass someone. When your wife stops nagging you, that's a sure sign she's having an affair and has found someone else to nag.

name your poison: to say what alcohol you would like to drink.

Usually the word 'beer' has come out of my mouth by the time someone's said, 'Name yo—'.

name-dropper: someone who casually mentions their encounters with famous people during a conversation.

People do this to try to impress everyone else but just end up looking like a wanker. Anyway, my good mate George Clooney said that name-dropping isn't cool.

nature strip: that narrow bit of grass between your house and the road.

Where you put your rubbish bins for emptying and where

your neighbour's bins end up after being emptied. Speaking of neighbours, they only ever mow their nature strip up to the exact point that divides the two properties. They never go over and mow a bit of yours. Some of them must get down on their knees and measure it with a ruler. I love how it's called a 'nature strip' even though, as far as I can see, other than some grass, there's very little nature on it at all. Unless, of course, a dog turd falls under the category of 'nature'.

need it like a hole in the head: when you don't want something.

It'd be a great line to say if someone was about to shoot you in the head. 'Great, I need that like a hole in the head.' No matter how angry they were, you'd probably at least get a giggle out of them.

newfangled: modern; the latest.

It could refer to anything from a kitchen appliance to a new electronic gadget, or in my case a newfangled artificial hip.

nice drop: a tasty drink.

Usually refers to wine. It's pretty weird seeing someone at a wine tasting take a swig, spit it out and then say, 'Nice drop!'

nick off: to leave quickly.

You can nick off or you can tell someone else to nick off. Telling someone to nick off is usually done in anger and makes you feel like Alf from *Home and Away*: 'Go on, nick off you flamin' mongrels!'

niggle: a worrying small pain in a muscle or joint that could lead to a more serious injury.

It may be a niggle in your ankle, knee or hamstring. Generally speaking, when a coach says their player has a niggle, you can guarantee it's more serious than that. I've now got a niggle in my finger from typing this stuff into the computer.

nineteenth hole: the bar in the golf course clubhouse.

Always the best hole that I play. Don't ever wear your cap into the nineteenth hole.

nipper: a kid; a young child who is at walking age.

They just love to hang off your legs, not realising that they could easily trip you up and be squashed beyond recognition if you landed on top of them.

no ball: illegal delivery in cricket.

What the entire crowd at the MCG yells out when Murali comes in to bowl. The most common 'no ball' is a result of the bowler's foot going over the line. This happens when he misjudges his run up or he is on the take and has to bowl a no ball at that particular time to keep his illegal bookmaker friend happy.

no dice: it ain't happening.

When you refuse to do something, usually for a good reason. It could be your response to an offer or a deal. In fact, they should change the name of that show to *Dice or No Dice*.

no flies on me: I've done something smart or clever.

You might have the answer to a question that's been bugging everyone or you could've come up with the solution to a problem. Once your genius has been on display for everyone to see, that's when you say, 'No flies on me!' And that's when someone else says, 'There's no flies on you but I can see where they've been.'

no news is good news: an expression to make yourself feel better when you don't hear from someone.

The theory being that whenever you hear news it's usually bad. Someone needs to tell the TV networks. All it seems they want to do these days is tell us as much news as they can, even if there isn't much around.

no oil painting: someone who's not particularly beautiful.

After having seen some of the oil paintings at the art gallery, who'd want to be one, anyway? Imagine looking like a Picasso. Who wants both eyes on the same side of their head? Or even that lady who doesn't smile . . . Lisa someone.

no strings attached: no obligation.

A relationship that is purely sexual. Sounds too good to be true, doesn't it? That's because it is. It's pretty rare for this to work without any bumps along the way. How good would it be, though, if it did work? . . . Um . . . not very good at all, I would think. Sounds like a stupid idea, right, Darl?

no wuckers: no worries; not a problem.

A way of reassuring someone that everything is okay. Another Aussie expression that makes overseas visitors really confused. So, if you see a tourist, make sure you use it a lot.

nod off: to fall asleep.

It's always funny watching someone nod off on the train. Their head gets heavy and then it falls forward, which immediately causes them to jolt it back up, only for it fall down again. This goes on and on for ages and for some reason it's fascinating. They eventually wake up and notice that everyone is staring at them, mainly because they're still dribbling. The embarrassment continues when they realise they've missed their stop. Some people can nod off almost anywhere. On the couch, on their lounge chair, on the beanbag, in front of the telly, on their desk at work, on a plane, while a passenger in a car, while driving a car, during love making (happened to me once. I think my drink was spiked), at the movies, in parliament, at a bar or even while exercising. The experts say that having a power nap is good for you. So, based on that theory, having four naps in a day must be four times as good for you. Yeah! Billy's doing just fine.

noggin: the head.
Personally, I reckon 'noggin' only applies to some heads. A big hard head is a noggin. That makes my head a noggin. Jonathan Brown's head would be a noggin. Cameron Mooney's head's a noggin. Dipper's head is a massive noggin. James Brayshaw's head? Mmm, too delicate and fluffy to be a noggin.

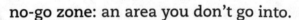

no-go zone: an area you don't go into.
Often refers to conversation. It could be a topic that is a bit sensitive or offensive. As soon as someone goes near it, someone else will pull them up and say, 'That's a no-go zone.' Then again it could be a small area in the backyard that you've roped off because you are trying to grow grass. Unfortunately, the dog has no concept of a no-go zone.

none the wiser: unaware; when you do something to someone and they never find out.
You could spill something on a co-worker's desk and then clean it up before they get back and they'd be none the wiser. Go on, try it tomorrow. Just don't spill anything that is too sticky.

non-event: something that isn't important or doesn't live up to expectations; an event where nowhere near enough people showed up.
When North play a home game against Freo.

norgs: boobs.
Generally great boobs.

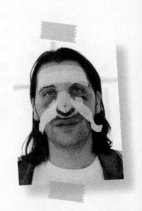

nose out of joint, to get your: to be upset about something.
If someone is not invited to a function, they might get their nose out of joint. If they try to force their way in then the bouncer might put their nose out of joint as well.

not all there: someone who is not the full quid.
This can be best explained by any one of the following: someone who is a couple of sandwiches short of a picnic. Someone who is not the full packet of biscuits. Someone who's not playing with a full deck. Someone who's a stubby short of a sixpack. Someone who's a few snags short of a barbie. Someone who's a few palings short of a fence. Someone who's a few French fries short of a happy meal. Someone whose lift doesn't go all the way to the top. I hope you're getting the idea now because I'm running out of these.

not my cup of tea: something you don't like.
It could be anything. Lots of things aren't my cup of tea, especially cups of tea. Can't stand 'em.

not on: not happening; unacceptable.
A pub running out of beer – that's not on. Me running out of beer at home – that's also not on.

not the end of the world: get over it; it's not that bad.
That saying has a long lifespan. The only time you couldn't use it would be if the earth collided with an asteroid and life on this planet as we knew it was no more. At which point you could probably get away with changing it to 'It's not the end of the universe.'

nothing in it: what you say at the AFL tribunal to help get a player off who belted you.

nous: smarts; brains.
There's no real way of measuring nous. You can only judge it on what you see people do. I do know how you can measure a complete lack of nous: when someone tries to cross the road and not use the pedestrian crossing that is only 10 metres down the road, or when someone rides their bike in the dark without lights or a helmet. I happened to see both those things within two minutes of each other one night. I nearly hit them. Fortunately, I was able to swerve, which was quite an achievement considering I was eating a burger and talking on the mobile at the same time. The Darl's got heaps of nous. She must have, she married me.

nude nut: bald head.
Gary Ablett Jnr. I'm well on my way too, there's no denying that. I do carry it well, though.

nude up: get your gear off; strip.
What I did when *The Footy Show* went to Germany. I took it one step further and ran around as well. I don't speak German but the vibe I was getting was that everyone thought it was great. Some were laughing a little too hard and pointing but I was in another country so I had to be polite.

nuggety: short and stocky with thick thighs and calves.

There have been some great nuggety AFL players over the years. Lethal Leigh Matthews for one. It's really hard for them to crack it in the big time these days because the draft camp is all about height, speed and jumping. Forget the rookie draft, we need the nuggety draft.

nunchaku: a traditional Japanese weapon made up of two wooden sticks connected by a chain or rope.

As seen in heaps of martial arts films. Often called nunchuks or nunchukas. They are considered a dangerous weapon and not available over the counter in this country. If you want to use them, you have to be playing a video game.

nungers: boobs.

Really big ones.

O is a blood type. Not sure if it is mine. I can't remember what mine is. Some experts say you should eat differently depending on what your blood type is. Fingers crossed my blood type needs dim sims and burgers. O is also the chemical symbol for oxygen, our most important element on earth. We need it to breathe. I'm guilty of using up more than my fair share. After I've been on a run, I suck the oxygen in at four times the rate of the average bloke. My favourite O was the Big O, Roy Orbison. He had some all-time classic songs, like 'Pretty Woman', 'Crying' and 'Only the Lonely'. The most amazing thing about his career was that he never fell off stage even though he was always wearing those dark glasses.

occy strap: a stretchy cord with hooks on both ends.

Used to tie stuff down on a trailer or on a car's roof racks. Ideal for people like me who aren't good at tying knots with rope.

The problem with occy straps is the constant worry that they're going to fling back and take someone's eye out with the hook.

ocker: Australian.

Very Australian. Drinking with mates, watching sport and generally being rowdy and unaware that you're annoying others. Hang on – that's me!

octopus: a bloke who has his hands all over the ladies to the point where they feel uncomfortable.

He usually ends up crawling away in pain after having been kicked in a sensitive area.

Octopus is not part of my seafood diet (see page 60) – it's too weird looking. I prefer calamari, crumbed. Let's face it, almost everything tastes better crumbed and fried.

odd jobs: little jobs that need to be done, often around the house.

The list at my place grows by the week. My theory is that if you wait long enough, then things get to a point where they're beyond repair and you don't have to worry about them.

odds-on: to have a very good chance of winning.

Can also apply to something that looks like it's very likely to happen. There are many cases where things that are odds-on to win somehow don't. Just ask the bloke with the big grin on his face who runs my local TAB.

off the hook: to escape from being in trouble.
Often because some other evidence has been brought to light that clears your name. You could also be off the hook if you were given a particular job to do but it has fallen through for some reason. If you were supposed to drive to the other side of town to pick someone up, but now they're coming home with someone else, you're off the hook. Unfortunately, you tend to find yourself more on the hook than off. Sometimes I take myself off the hook, walk away and wait to see if anyone has noticed.

off your face: drunk.
Been there on the odd occasion. By 'odd' I mean every second day.

off your game: not playing well.
For some reason, you're not playing at your usual level. It could be due to any number of things. You could be feeling sick, carrying an injury, have something on your mind or you just plain couldn't be stuffed one day. I was so far off my game one day that when I stopped and had a look, I realised I'd been running around in the car park.

off-load: get rid of something.
You usually don't want it because it is either damaged, dangerous or has been superseded. Someone may have off-loaded something on you that you now want to off-load on someone else. Eventually, it will find its way back to you. It always does.

oil: information that has been passed on to you from a reliable source.

It could be the good oil on a race horse or a footballer's injury. Oil also refers to the stuff you put in your car engine to make it run smoothly. It needs to be regularly replaced, as my mechanic informed me after my engine blew up.

old bomb: an old car that is falling apart.

At some stage in our lives most of us have driven an old bomb. There's nothing like the feeling of being miles away from home, hopping into your car and praying that it will start. I had an old bomb – we used to call it the bandwagon because everyone would jump on it.

old codger: an old man who you may be having issues with.

We'll all get old one day and we need to show respect to the elderly. But it doesn't give them a licence to abuse the rest of us. It doesn't happen very often but when it does and an old codger decides to cause trouble you need to take the appropriate action. Nothing a tranquilliser dart can't fix.

old flame: a past girlfriend.

You often bump into them at a really inopportune moment. Like when you're single and they've got a new boyfriend who's better looking and richer than you.

old hat: something you used to do or used to like that has gone out of style.

Usually I'm still doing it until someone tells me that it's old hat. At which point, I can't wait to tell someone else that it's old hat.

old lady: Mum.

old man: Dad.

old stamping ground: a place you used to hang out.
Often refers to bars or nightclubs you went to on a regular basis. It's hard for me to have old stamping grounds because I never stopped going to them.

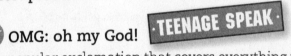

These **oldies** are probably **over the hill** when it comes to hanky panky (see page 80). Then again, they both look pretty happy with their **other half**.

oldies: parents.

 OMG: oh my God! TEENAGE SPEAK
Very popular exclamation that covers everything from *I've just bought a new pair of shoes at half price* to *I've just had my arm amputated in an accident.*

on ice: put on hold; waiting.
My football comeback has been on ice for fifteen years.

on the blink: not working; broken.
Best used when referring to a fridge or a TV. 'The fridge is on the blink' sounds right. The words 'blink' and 'fridge' go together, whereas, 'The microwave is on the blink' doesn't quite work for me.

on the level: open and honest.
Whenever someone makes you a good offer or if they're giving you some important information, you need to make

sure they're on the level. You usually do this by asking them if they're on the level. Which is pretty silly because if they weren't on the level in the first place, they're not going to all of a sudden pop up and say that they've been having you on the whole time.

on the nose: something's just not right.
Approach with caution. Sometimes a deal is too good to be true and that's when you start getting suspicious. It stinks. Smells funny. On the other hand, you may have just stood in doggy do and that's what is really on the nose.

on the rebound: jumping onto the next thing after a relationship break-up.
The end of a long-term relationship can be pretty traumatic. This will often result in a person becoming desperate to be with anybody, which really suits others who have never been in a relationship at all and are desperate to be with anybody as well. Ah, two desperate people . . . it's just gotta work, right?

on the receiving end: to cop the full brunt of an action.
I was on the receiving end heaps of times on the football field. A player would get angry, look around for the nearest bloke to whack and I always happened to be the one standing there. Sometimes it was even my own teammates who let fly on me. It got to the stage where I had to ask the club if I could wear padding like the goalposts, to which someone replied, 'You may as well, you're about as agile as a goalpost.' I took offence at that once I went home and looked up what the word 'agile' meant.

on the sly: doing something in a dodgy and secretive way.
Taking cash money for work or doing extra work on the side without the boss knowing. Yep, so I'm pretty much including most Australians here.

on the spot: without hesitation; immediately.
The police often give you an on-the-spot fine for a traffic offence. I always offer to pay it on the spot with cash. They're usually not very impressed. They claim that's called a bribe. Then I have to explain to them that I wasn't winking as I handed the money over, I actually had something stuck in my eye. What a mix-up.

on the take: when a person in a position of authority or power accepts money or gifts to help someone out.
It's been going on forever. Whenever a country wins the rights to host the Olympics or the World Cup, rumours start flying around that they paid money to people on the committees to get the bid over the line. There are also stories of buildings and major constructions getting approved because local councils have been on the take. The sad thing is I couldn't even get a permit to put up a shed. Sure it was 14-metres square and two storeys high but technically it was still a shed.

one for the road: to have one last beer before leaving.
Often you'll go to leave and your mates will say, 'Come on, one more for the road.' There's something in our culture and tradition that somehow means you're obliged to stay for another drink. Your mates know that you can't refuse. If you really put your mind to it, you can find ways around it. Instead of driving, catch public transport to the pub. 'One for the train' just doesn't have the same ring to it and definitely won't compel you to stay for another drink.

one-armed bandit: poker machine.
They don't have a lever now so they're pretty much armless bandits. They're all computerised and you press a button or many buttons, depending on how many lines you want to bet on and the amount you want to bet. They also make great sounds to bamboozle and hypnotise you. Music plays, the screen flashes, you get excited, and people gather around as you discover that you've only won five dollars.

one-eyed: being biased towards your own team.
Football supporters are very one-eyed, especially Collingwood fans. I'm a one-eyed Cats supporter and I'm not ashamed of that. When they won the premiership I cried in front of millions of viewers and I'm not embarrassed about that at all. Trust me, I've done far more embarrassing things. I'm just glad the cameras weren't there to capture those.

one-night stand: sleeping with someone you met that night.
Nothing ever comes of it and you just go your separate ways. If both people are happy with that, then no harm has been done ... unless you weren't wearing protection, in which case, any number of things could have happened that may or may not require a trip to the doctor.

other half: wife, girlfriend or Siamese twin.

out of pocket: how much money you've spent or lost on a deal or purchase.
You could've gone in with a few people to buy someone a present but one of the group didn't pay up, so whoever paid for

the present is out of pocket. In that case, you don't let the person sign the card until they've paid up. Then again, most blokes buying a present don't worry about a card, so I may have to rethink that one.

outie: a bellybutton that sticks out.
Looks a lot weirder than an innie (a bellybutton that goes in). The biggest bummer about having an outie is that you've got nowhere to rest an egg that you've boiled and want to start eating.

over the hill: past it; getting too old.
I'm not over the hill yet but I can see the hill up ahead and it's calling me. Luckily, there are a few pubs on the way to slow me down.

P. Diddy dropped the 'P' and just became Diddy because, according to him, 'It was getting between me and my fans.' I hope his fans appreciated that. Not many performers are prepared to change their name, so that their fans can get closer to them. Not sure how that works, so I'll keep moving. P-platers are newly licensed drivers on our roads. In Victoria they have to be on their red Ps for one year and their green Ps for three years. It's good that the rest of us know who they are. That way we get to yell out, 'Bloody P-plater!' even when they haven't done anything wrong. Some people can't wait to get off their P-plates. Others are too lazy to even take off the P-plates when they no longer need them. I've been a P-plater for 22 years.

pa: grandfather.
Some grandfathers don't want to be called 'Grandpa' because it makes them feel old. They tell their grandchildren to call them 'Pa' instead. My grandpa was losing his hearing, so we'd call him anything we liked.

packed: full; chockers.
Nothing beats playing in front of a packed stadium. Unless it's the MCG and it's grand final day and you lose for the fourth time.

packin': to be scared; really afraid.
It's okay to be packin'. It's a very Australian thing to be. It's much cooler to be packin' than to be scared, even though they mean exactly the same thing.

pads: protective cricket wear for your legs.
The second-most important piece of cricket equipment. The first, of course, being the box, which protects your private parts. I'm not normally one to brag, but in my case, I need a pad to protect me there as well.

panic merchant: someone who regularly hits the panic button even over small things.
There's one in every workplace and everyone around them can't help but fuel the panic, so they can sit back and watch it

get worse. Not in a bad way. You need to keep the workplace interesting and entertaining. Okay, maybe it is in a bad way.

pants someone: to pull down another person's pants.
Still not sure why we find this so

amusing but we do. If someone is wearing tracky-dacks, it's only a matter of time before a mate pulls those down. Sometimes, without meaning to, you pull down the undies as well, which can take something that was going to be funny and turn it into something really awkward and embarrassing, especially if that bloke's family is there . . . but we're still prepared to take that risk.

pardon my French (see also, excuse the French): excusing yourself before or after you swear.

Not sure why it's not 'pardon my German' or 'pardon my Romanian', but I'm happy to go with what everyone else wants to. I did use the expression the other day. I was at Bakers Delight and I said, 'Pardon my French, but can I get a croissant, please.'

party animal: someone with a reputation for partying hard.

Some of my mates are party animals. We'll go out and they'll want me to kick on with them till all hours of the morning. I end up doing it every time. That doesn't make me a party animal. I'm just tagging along with the party animals, that's different. Yes, Billy, you keep trying to convince yourself. Good luck with that.

party pooper: someone who is intent on ruining a party.

You know the one. The person who always wants to turn down the music or tell people to behave themselves. The person who calls the police to come and stop the party and clear everyone out. Sure, it was 4 a.m. and it was at her house and those of us left didn't know the lady that well, but what a party pooper.

pass the buck: to blame someone else for a problem you've caused.

Happens at work all the time because people don't want to look stupid or lose their job. They'd rather someone else looked stupid and lost their job. If you pass the buck too often you'll eventually get found out. I do it at home all the time, but there's only so much mess you can blame on the kids. When the form guide and empty stubbies are strewn across the couch, it's not too hard to work out who left them there. Not to be confused with that other saying 'pass the Bucks', which is a party game involving passing around a former Collingwood champ.

> They should change this saying to 'pass the ice-cream container around' or 'pass the envelope' because that's what it often is.

pass the hat around: to collect money for someone's present.

Usually done at work when someone is leaving. It's always interesting because the amount of money collected depends on how popular the person is. It can be pretty embarrassing at someone's farewell party when, on behalf of their work-mates, you're giving them a voucher for the two-dollar shop. I suppose you're not going to see them again, so who cares, hey?

Pat Malone: rhyming slang for being alone.

Sometimes shortened to 'Pat'. 'I'm on my Pat.' One of the few rhyming slang terms that is still used a fair bit today. Always good to go for a beer on your Pat Malone. Makes for a cheap shout.

pav: pavlova or Matthew Pavlich, Fremantle's captain in the AFL.

Pavlova is one of my favourite desserts. Matthew Pavlich isn't as tasty but he's probably still very nutritious.

pay the price: to suffer for having done something wrong.

I paid the price for letting myself go a bit after my football career finished. I went a bit hard and consumed a fair few frothies. Then again, I've had a pretty good time so I haven't paid that much. In fact, I think I'm in front by a couple of bucks.

pea brain: an idiot; someone of low intelligence.

Feels really good to say. Go on, try it. Call the nearest thing a pea brain, even if it's the toaster, it'll still feel good. See, I told you.

peeved: angry; upset.

Not full-on angry and upset, though, more a watered-down version. If someone punches you in the face, you're going to be a bit more than just peeved about it. So peeved is like being half angry – not really worth the effort, is it? If you're going to be angry, you may as well go all the way, I say. I'm getting peeved right now just thinking about it. So, being peeved does have a purpose. Confused? That makes two of us!

pen-pusher: someone who works in an office.

It's our way of belittling them. Remember, just be careful what you say to a pen-pusher because they're holding something they can very easily stab you with.

pep talk: a talk to fire someone up; words of encouragement to make someone perform better.

Pep talks are great to give. I give pep talks to random people I see when I'm walking down the street. For instance, the guy in the fruit shop: 'Come on, mate. You can sell more bananas than that. I know you can!' It gives him a burst of energy and before you know it, bananas are flying out the door, most of them in my direction as I run off.

perve: to stare.

Especially at chicks. As a bloke it's hard not to; it must be some in-built thing we have. If it goes beyond a little look and you find yourself staring for a while, then maybe you should stop because it can make the person you're staring at feel very uncomfortable. Then you can be labelled as a perve, and you'll be stuck with that tag for life. I think they actually have to put it on your licence.

pet hate: the thing that annoys you the most.

My pet hate is people who press the button at the pedestrian crossing and then walk across before the lights have gone red to stop the traffic. If you're going to make cars stop, at least make them feel like they're stopping for a reason. You can't have it both ways! I'm doing the right thing, sitting in my car and waiting patiently at the red light while no one is crossing the road because they already did two minutes ago. Those few minutes are very valuable to me. I could drink a couple of frothies in that time.

PhD: a fancy qualification.

Everyone has a PhD in hindsight, and don't they love telling you what you should've done when it's all over. The only answer is, 'Thanks Captain Obvious.'

pick a fight: to start an argument with someone.

Can often end in the two parties coming to blows. I'm not the type to do this. Well, not on purpose anyway. In the past I may have been a bit careless with my words and offended some-one, or after a few beers not realised that my big frame was invading the space of others, but that is just me having a good time and forgetting that there are people around me. Usually I can talk my way out of it by being my loveable, cuddly self. What can I say, it's a gift. I'm certainly not one to go look-ing for trouble. The main reason being that I would probably get my head punched in. Well, that and the fact that I don't really get the whole fighting thing. The sound of fist on face is one of the most unpleasant noises you'll ever hear. We're all just skin and bone and we can get hurt. Every week you read a story in the paper about a bloke who died after being hit with one punch. Someone who got knocked out, smashed their head on the ground and never woke up. Punching on rarely solves a problem; it just makes for a bigger problem. It's nowhere near as much fun as they make it look in the movies.

pick-up line: a line used to pick up a chick.

They're known for their cringe-worthiness. Fortunately, my charm was always enough to get me through, but a lot of my mates struggled in that department and found themselves having to rely on pick-up lines. Most of which were pretty embarrassing and, I'm sad to say, are still doing the rounds. Here is a random selection of ten pick-up lines for you to look at and use if you are desperate. Some are cheesy, some make me laugh, but most are pretty bad:

- If I could rearrange the alphabet, I'd put 'U' and 'I' together.
- You must be in the wrong place. The Miss Universe contest is next door.

- If you were a new burger at McDonald's, you'd be the McGorgeous.
- You know what? Your eyes are the same colour as my Porsche.
- I'm new in town. Do you think you can give me directions to your place?
- I've just moved you to the top of my 'to do' list.
- Were you arrested earlier? It's got to be illegal to look that good.
- My love for you is like diarrhoea: I just can't hold it in.
- Can I buy you a drink or do you just want the money?
- Well, here I am. What were your other two wishes?

pig in shit, happy as a: very happy.
Me, during happy hour.

pig out: to eat too much.

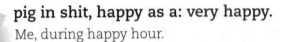

Something we all do at Christmas time. You don't like to do it too often but some of these 'all you can eat' restaurants (not sure if the use of the term 'restaurant' is quite appropriate) make it really hard for you not to pig out. If the food is there and it needs to be eaten, then who am I to stand in the way of fate. When you do tell someone that you 'pigged out', you need to tap your belly twice or rub it as you speak. We all have to add that bit for some reason.

piggyback: to carry someone on your back.
Only recommended if the person you're carrying is smaller than you. Great fun was had piggybacking each other as kids but then it disappeared. That is, until your wife or girlfriend can't walk in her heels any more and you end up having to piggyback her to the car or even home. No matter how heavy

she gets, you can't let on. The pain of carrying her is far more preferable than the pain of the earful you'll cop for suggesting that she's too heavy to carry.

pills: testicles.

pipe down: be quiet; stop talking; shut up.
When your kids are making too much noise, you'll often stick your head in the door and tell them to 'pipe down'. It rarely makes any difference. Come to think of it, it's a fairly old saying, so maybe they've got no idea what it means.

piss: urine and/or beer.
I can't believe it somehow became acceptable to use this word for both. One is my favourite beverage, the other my least favourite beverage. Despite this, we never get confused when someone uses the word. If a mate says, 'I was out all night on the piss' we know exactly what he means. I think. I do have one mate I'm not quite sure about.

piss off: get lost; go away.
Can be directed at people, dogs, cats, flies and even the rain. You've got to love an expression that is so versatile.

pissed off: angry; infuriated.
When we do get pissed off, we love telling other people that we're pissed off: 'I'm pissed off!' Others don't really care, but by saying it you start to feel better.

pisser: something funny; something that really made you laugh.
'That joke was a pisser!' 'When he fell over it was a pisser!' 'Billy's book is a pisser!'

piss-farting around: mucking around; wasting time.
Personally, I consider it an art form. One I've spent years fine-tuning, to the point where I now consider myself to be one of the best exponents of piss-farting around in the country. If only they had piss-farting around world championships, I could've been somebody.

pissing into the wind: wasting your time; attempting to do something that is pointless.
Going to a lot of trouble and just getting nowhere. None of which could possibly be anywhere near as bad as actually pissing into a strong breeze.

WELCOME

piss-up: an organised big drinking session.
Can only go one way really. A lot of sore heads the next morning. The thing about most piss-ups is that the alcohol is usually the only thing that is taken care of. Other important things, like food and transport, aren't given much thought. Not that anyone really cares on the night, especially after their fifth or sixth drink. They're having way too much fun to worry about anything except their next drink. Just writing this is making me want to organise a big piss-up. Who's with me?

piss-weak: not good enough; a poor effort.
A very harsh criticism of someone's performance, one nobody wants to hear. I may have heard it once or twice . . . per game.

plastered: drunk.

play around: to cheat on your partner.
By calling it 'playing around' it doesn't sound as bad as it really is. Let's face it, you're doing a lot more than just playing

around. A lot of blokes can't help themselves. They see a chick and they just go for it without thinking about the consequences. All I can say is that there's no such thing as a free lunch. I've had a few lunches in my time, so I know what I'm talking about.

play chicken: to do something dangerous as a dare.

Most commonly used when referring to the risky practice of standing in front of an oncoming car and trying to make it swerve. Not a sport you're going to have longevity in.

play hard to get: to ignore the advances of someone who is trying to hit on you.

I've found it always works. The more uninterested you are, the more desperate they are to have you. I played hard to get with the Darl. After we met I didn't call her for ages. I'd actually lost her phone number, but it worked a treat.

plonk: wine, generally of the cheap variety.

Nothing better than sitting down to dinner with a nice bottle of plonk. Also means to put down or to sit down. So you can plonk yourself down and enjoy a bottle of plonk.

Plugger: Tony Lockett.

Former St Kilda and Sydney footballer. Probably the greatest full-forward ever. He holds the record for the most goals kicked in AFL history at 1360. He's won numerous Coleman medals, is the only full-forward to win the Brownlow medal and is a member of the AFL Hall of Fame. I was lucky enough to play in games against him, one of the best being the 1991 elimination final at Waverley, where we beat the Saints by 7 points, even though Plugger kicked nine goals. My eight goals may have helped us but this is about Plugger not me! He now breeds and races greyhounds and is

very good at it. He was a crowd-puller in his day but now pre-
fers a quiet life away from the limelight, but I'll never forget
those eight goals I kicked . . . I mean the nine goals he kicked
in that final.

pollies: politicians.
The people we trust the least yet who we give
the power to run the country.

Pom: someone from England.

Pommyland: England.

pop the question: to ask someone to marry you.
I strongly suggest you're 99.9 per cent sure what the answer
will be before you ask. The hardest part about it all is asking
her father first. Make sure he's not holding a stubby or anything else he can hurt you with. People often ask a couple
where the proposal took place. I just say that I proposed at the
doctors when I found out she was pregnant.

porky: a little white lie. Nothing too serious.
Also a great film (*Porky's*, 1982) and two sequels.

pot: a big glass of beer.
If the first shout was in pots, don't even think about buying
your round in standard glasses. A pot also refers to a big gut
that sticks out, which can be caused by drinking too many pots.

power nap: a sleep you have during the day because you're knackered.
There's nothing worse than waking up from a
sleep during the day. You have no idea what
time it is, where you are and who you are.

After panicking for the first twenty seconds, you soon realise that it's all okay and that you're not late for work. You then try to get up and your whole body feels like it's in a different time zone. You feel like you need a jolt of electricity through you in order to get going again . . . and they call that a power nap!

power-walking: when you walk a bit faster than normal.

A lot of chicks do it to keep fit. Some do it while they're shopping, which is quite an impressive thing to watch and very difficult to keep up with.

prima donna: someone who prances around like they deserve some sort of special treatment.

They think that they're better than everyone else and get really upset when they want something. A knockabout bloke like me hasn't got much time for prima donnas. I'll usually tell them to pull their head in. If they don't listen to me, then it won't be long before someone else knocks their head off.

privates: genitals.

pub: a place to drink beer, usually has a bar, some beer and me in it.

A great place to meet friends and strangers alike. A very important building. Most small towns even have one. I don't know how we'd survive without them; I'm starting to tear up now.

pub crawl: going to a number of pubs in the one day.

At least one beer must be consumed at each pub, sometimes more. In most cases it is very well organised. The pubs that will be visited are usually known in advance. It's a massive day, with some blokes dropping out along the way, and a real test of stamina and staying power. Probably best not to go home that night; you'll be in no condition to be of any use there.

puke: to spew up.
A very common occurrence on a pub crawl. The word 'puke' sounds very much like the noise you make when you throw up.

pump someone up: to fill someone with confidence; to offer encouragement to someone, especially if they're feeling down.
Seen a lot in sport. Sometimes you need to pump someone up to get the best out of them. I used to pump up my teammates and tell them how good they were. This, hopefully, would result in them kicking the ball to me a bit more.

punt: to bet.
To take a chance on something or in my case, lose your shirt.

puppy fat: some extra weight you have when you're younger that disappears as you get older.
In my case, it must have been hiding in the garage, waiting to attach itself to me again.

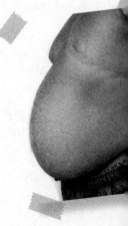

pussy cats: Geelong football team.
The best. Go Cats!

put down: an insult.
To humiliate someone with a cutting remark. Comedians use these to deal with hecklers. Here are some examples:

• Next time you shave try standing a centimetre or two closer to the blade.

- Are you always this stupid or are you making a special effort today?
- As an outsider what do you think of the human race?
- I'm guessing you're better at sex than anyone. Now, you just need a partner.
- You're depriving a village somewhere of an idiot.
- Were you the first person in your family born without a tail?
- What colour is the sky in your world?
- You are down to earth. Unfortunately, you're not quite far down enough.
- If your brain was chocolate, it would fill an M&M.
- You're so stupid, you could throw a rock at the ground and miss.

Q is the bloke in the James Bond movies who looks after all the gadgets. It would've been really handy having Q down at Geelong when I was playing footy there. I could've had specially made boots that'd release a smokescreen out the back so that I could lose my opponent. Then again, that was something I could achieve by having a couple of cans of baked beans before the game. 'Q and A', means questions and answers. There's no worse feeling than when your partner wants to sit down for a bit of Q and A. Hopefully she's talking about the show *Q and A* on the ABC, which can be either really interesting or so boring that you want to scratch your own eyes out.

QANTAS: our national airline.

It used to really confuse me that there was no 'U' after the 'Q' until I found out that it stands for Queensland and North-ern Territory Aerial Services.

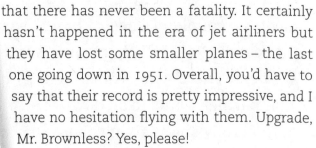

If only they'd called it Queensland 'United' and Northern Territory Aerial Services, then it wouldn't have messed with so many of our minds. QANTAS is well known for its safety record. We are often reminded how QANTAS has never had an accident. It is even referred to in the movie *Rain Man*. I hate to sound like a party pooper but it isn't true that QANTAS planes have never crashed, and that there has never been a fatality. It certainly hasn't happened in the era of jet airliners but they have lost some smaller planes – the last one going down in 1951. Overall, you'd have to say that their record is pretty impressive, and I have no hesitation flying with them. Upgrade, Mr. Brownless? Yes, please!

quad: quadriceps.

Muscles in your upper leg, which you can strain while playing sport. You don't seem to get as much sympathy when you've done a quad as when you've done your hammy. It's also a little bit weirder having a trainer massage the front of your thigh than the back.

quaddie: a type of bet.

It involves you picking the four winners of four nominated races on the same day. Not an easy thing to do but if you pull one off, it usually means a big win. If some strange bloke at the races just comes up and gives you a bottle of Champagne, chances are he just won the quaddie. There's nothing more frustrating than getting three legs of the quaddie and your horse in the fourth leg getting beaten by a nose. In fact, 'frustrating' is too soft a term to use – you go absolutely bananas when that happens. You just want to smash stuff. Gambling's fun though. Yep, heaps of fun.

quadrangle: that concrete or bitumen area at school, usually between classrooms, where you'd play ball games at lunchtime and recess.

This is where we learned to be tough, take knocks, weasel our way out of things and stand up for ourselves. These represent all the skills and traits needed by us blokes as we got older. I wouldn't mind getting the boys together for a game of four square or downball for old time's sake. Every time you'd go out, you'd yell 'inter!' (interference) but it rarely saved you, no matter how hard you argued that an out-of-control soccer ball got too close to you and impeded your ability to hit the tennis ball back.

Queen: great band.

'We are the Champions' is played after a sporting team wins a grand final at any level and 'Bohemian Rhapsody' is an absolute classic. The late Freddie Mercury was one of the most charismatic lead singers of all time. Also an old lady who has corgies.

Quentin Tarantino: American filmmaker, writer, director, producer and occasional actor.

He revolutionised movies with his dialogue-driven scripts and over-the-top violence. Some of his more successful films include *Pulp Fiction*, *Kill Bill* 1 and 2 and *Inglourious Basterds*. He left school at fifteen and worked in a video store. He studied movies closely and this gave him his background and interest in directing. He's done pretty well for a bloke with the first name Quentin.

question mark: anything or anyone that has a degree of uncertainty about them.

If a football player is still injured and in doubt for a game then there is a question mark over him. When those new low-carb beers came out, there was a question mark over them. They seem to be selling all right but I say stop messing with the beer! Leave my carbs in there, thanks. Pretty soon they'll have a new light, low-carb, cold-filtered, transparent ale or as we know it better – water!

quick sticks: fast.

Get it done in a hurry. Something your dad would say when he wanted you to get a job done quickly, often resulting in you doing it too quickly and then being told off by him for not doing it properly.

quickie: a short love-making session.

It often happens in an unusual place, which could be anywhere from the car to a toilet cubicle to the photocopying room at work. If you've never had one, then there are three suggestions for you right there. Thanks, Billy! Don't mention it.

quid: money.

If you're doing well in business, then you're making a few quid. There are also some things that are so bad you wouldn't do them for quids, and some people aren't the full quid. I hope this book makes a quid.

quiz: the questions the Darl asks when you get home plastered.

Feels like you're on *It's Academic* but there are no prizes and no multiple choice answers. Hey, there's an idea. Instead of impossible-to-answer questions it could go like this, where you just have to choose a, b or c.

Where have you been?
a) at the pub
b) at the TAB
c) at [mate's] place

Why are you so late?
a) I ran into one of Dad's old mates
b) I didn't have my watch
c) I had to finish the shout

What's that lipstick on your collar?
a) It's not my shirt
b) I ran into my sister
c) It's the publican's wife's birthday

R&R refers to rest and recreation. Something we all need and something I really love. For my rest and recreation I like to get away. I don't care where, as long as it's away. It doesn't need to be anywhere special, as long as I can read the paper, watch a bit of telly, have a beer and sit by a pool. If I can do all of those things at the same time, even better. When you go to school there are the three Rs: reading, riting and rithmetic. I was good at the fourth R – rudely interrupting the teacher.

rabbit food: salad.

Whenever you see a bloke having a lunch that's got a lot of lettuce in it, you give him a hard time for not having meat. You then hoe into your meat pie – not that it has much meat in it either.

rabble: a group in disarray.

When a sporting team is getting badly beaten and is unable to get anything going, they're a rabble. Some teams can be a rabble for a number of years in a row. That's not an easy thing to do.

rack off: get lost; nick off.

It's pretty harsh, so it shouldn't be said to colleagues but can be said to people who knock on your front door trying to sell you stuff.

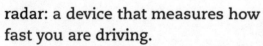

keep an old tennis racquet on hand. It can be useful to wave around to threaten kids who are making a racket.

racket: noise.

Kids are good at making a racket, especially when you're trying to sleep. As I tell my kids, when the adults have friends around that's not making a racket. It's called indulging in intelligent conversation over a few beers.

radar: a device that measures how fast you are driving.

The police point it at your car and if you are over the speed limit, you will be issued with a fine. The next step is to put the fine in your glove box and forget about it until you get a final warning letter. Why do the police have state-of-the-art radar guns for detecting speed yet the hand-guns they carry in their holsters look as if they're from the 1920s.

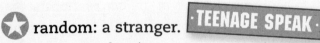 **random: a stranger.**
As in, 'Some random just came up to me.' It also means bringing something into a conversation that doesn't seem related to what you were talking about. You'll immediately get the response, 'Random!'

random breath test: a test conducted by police on drivers to determine how much alcohol is in their system.
The police make you blow into a device that measures the alcohol in your breath. The police will often do this by putting a booze bus on the side of the road and stopping heaps of motorists over a few hours. They usually pick a spot where they can't be seen until you come over a hill or around a corner. That way, people can't avoid being tested, unless of course they pull over, get out of their car, run off and swim across a river.

rapt: excited; happy.
You can be rapt with something in particular. 'Our team was rapt with that win.' 'I was rapt to find an extra potato cake in my fish and chips.'

rat's tail: a thin lock of hair that hangs a little longer than the rest.
Not the best look, especially on a kid. If I could actually grow some hair, I may have a different view on this.

razzle-dazzle: colour and excitement.
There is always a bit of razzle-dazzle at the grand final. Some players have a bit of razzle-dazzle about them. Not me. I was more frazzle-dazzle.

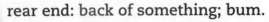

rear end: back of something; bum.

You can be rear-ended if someone crashes into the back of your car or you can rear-end someone else. The saying, 'It's better to give than to receive' doesn't apply here.

reckon: to think something.

Doesn't 100 per cent lock you in to that thought. You only 'reckon'; you don't absolutely guarantee or fully support it. That's why 'reckon' is one of the great Aussie words. 'I reckon it might rain today.' If there's no rain, it doesn't matter. I didn't say it was definitely going to rain. I'm going to use 'reckon' a lot more now, it's a beauty!

red: red wine.

Even though I'm a beer man, I can still appreciate a good red and Australian wines are popular throughout the world. We have some great wine-growing regions in every state of Australia. The more well-known being Margaret River, Barossa Valley, McLaren Vale, Heathcote, Yarra Valley, Hunter Valley and the Mornington Peninsula. Different regions are known for different wines. McLaren Vale produces great shiraz, as does Heathcote. The Mornington Peninsula has given us some great pinot noirs. You also don't need to spend a fortune to get a decent red. It's just a matter of trying a few and you'll soon discover what you like. I could say a lot more here but I don't want to come across as one of those wine wankers.

red carpet: what you walk up when you go somewhere special.

The Brownlow used to have a red carpet but they changed it to a blue one to keep the sponsor happy. Thankfully, the Brownlow's not sponsored by M&Ms.

red light: traffic signal.

Also the symbol for a brothel. Where there are a number of brothels in the one area, it is known as a red-light district. Where there are a lot of red traffic lights in an area, it is known as a pain in the arse.

red tape: rules and regulations that slow down any process.

There is a lot of red tape in government departments, which makes it really hard to get anything done. There's a lot of red tape in my house. I've got to put three submissions in to the Darl before I can get anything to happen.

red-faced: embarrassed.

If you get caught out having done the wrong thing then you'll be left *red-faced*. I've been left red-faced on a number of occasions. It's not an easy thing to do to go back to a venue the next day to ask if anyone has seen your pants.

red-light camera: a camera installed at traffic lights to catch motorists running a red light.

If a car has a close call as it goes through a red light, someone in the car will always say, 'Smile for the camera!'

rego: car registration.

One of my least favourite bills because you're not really sure what you're actually paying for. Six hundred dollars for a sticker, yippee!

regular: someone who goes back to the same place on a regular basis, especially a pub.

Sure, I'm a regular and I'm not ashamed of that. I also highly recommend the seven pubs I'm a regular at.

rellies: relatives.

Some people really struggle to spend time with their rellies and end up leaving before it gets ugly. Then again, what's a family gathering without an all-in brawl?

Richard Cranium: dickhead.

It's us blokes thinking that we've come up with a clever way of saying dickhead because 'Dick' is short for Richard and cranium means 'head'. If you have to explain this to the person you're calling Richard Cranium, then you've probably lost the impact of your original insult.

ring-in: a substitute.

Usually brought in at the last minute. In local or social sport, teams may have a ring-in who is of a higher standard than everyone else. That can be very frustrating for the opposition. There was a famous horseracing ring-in incident when a thoroughbred called Fine Cotton was replaced by a faster horse. It's a fascinating story that happened in 1984 at Eagle Farm Racecourse in Brisbane. Fine Cotton had a poor record. It had come tenth in a field of twelve in its previous race and was starting this race at odds of 33–1. The scam began when a syndicate of blokes purchased a Fine Cotton look-alike so that they could make a switch-a-roo and run off with the cash. Unfortunately, that horse was injured, so, having already invested, they quickly found another horse, called Bold Personality. The only problem they had now was that the two horses were different colours. Fine Cotton was a brown gelding with white markings on its legs, whereas Bold Personality was a bay gelding with no markings. They tried to apply hair colouring but that didn't quite work. They then painted the white markings on Bold Personality's legs. Racing officials were already suspicious before the horses jumped because of all the money that was on Fine Cotton. It had come in to 7–2. In a close finish, Fine Cotton (Bold Personality) won by a nose. As it returned to scale, like a scene from a comedy movie, paint was running down its legs. The horse was disqualified and an immediate investigation was launched. A number of racing identities were charged and punished. Some even went to jail. What a story! It makes you wonder if anyone was smart enough to ever pull something like that off. I suppose we'll never know.

rip-off: something that is not good value for money.
Like food at the footy. How can a hotdog be double the price just because it is on the other side of a concrete wall?

ripper: a good thing.
A person or a situation can be a ripper. Even writing about it now, I've realised that I don't hear it being used anywhere near as much as I used to. That's a shame. I'm making it my mission to do what I can to revive the term 'ripper', and I ask you to help me. Between us we should be able to ensure its survival. I want my grandchildren to be saying, 'You little ripper!'

road rage: an argument with another motorist.
Generally worth avoiding because it can get pretty ugly. It's important to avoid confrontation, so whatever you do, don't get out of your car, unless, of course, the other person has set your car on fire – then you'd better get out.

rock bottom: the lowest you can go.
Your team can hit rock bottom, the stock market can hit rock

bottom, your life can hit rock bottom. Hopefully you haven't experienced any of the above. Rock bottom isn't a good place to be at any time. It's generally a long way up from there. Those who have hit rock bottom and managed to get back up to the top again have achieved something special. Sometimes it takes you hitting rock bottom before you can appreciate anything. I've now exhausted my quota for the use of the word 'bottom' in this book.

roll with the punches: to take the good with the bad; to tolerate things.

Whatever comes your way, you deal with it. I always try to roll with the punches but end up walking into too many.

Roller: Rolls Royce.

A ridiculously expensive car. I wish they never existed. Why? Because I'm never, ever going to be able to afford one and I spend my whole time on the road hoping I don't hit one.

Rolls: Rolls Royce.

Get 'em off the road, I say.

Rolls Royce: car.

I think you all know how I feel about them. Also used to describe the best version of something. Nathan Buckley was the Rolls Royce at Collingwood. Another not-so-classy player might be called a Datsun 120Y.

Roos: North Melbourne Football Club.

JB's team. He swans around as if he owns them. Come to think of it, he probably could afford to buy them.

rooted: tired.

How you feel after you've played a game of football. If you happened to have had a bad loss, you'll feel even more rooted the next day when you're doing an early-morning training session. If something is broken it can also be 'rooted'. My lawnmower wouldn't start because it was rooted. I rang the lawnmower-repair guy but he couldn't fix it because his hand was rooted.

ropeable: angry; really pissed off.

I was ropeable when someone hit my car while it was parked and didn't leave their details. I made a very loud announcement to everyone who was in the car park at the time: 'I don't know which one of you did this but mark my words, I will find out!' They initially stopped and listened, but then just turned around and went about their business. Hopefully, one of them didn't sleep well that night.

 rouge: make-up that is applied to the cheeks.

I'm assuming it's the cheeks on the face but nothing would surprise me.

rough trot: when things aren't going well.

Not sure exactly what time span it covers. One morning I got up, accidentally kicked the bottom of the bed, tripped and whacked my head on the dresser and caught my pyjama top on a knob. The top ripped and my falling weight snapped off the knob. I went through a rough trot in the space of five seconds.

roughing it: going without the normal comforts of home.

When you go camping, you're roughing it. When you have a massive night out and wake up in a park somewhere, you're roughing it.

round: a round of drinks.

A drink is bought for everyone in your shout. The key is not to go too late in the shout. Everyone starts on beers but seven beers later, they might want to jump on to the spirits. It gets to your shout and it's bourbons and Coke all round. You end up paying twice as much for a shout as the blokes who went before you.

rubbed out: suspended.

When you have been punished due to an unwarranted act in a game of sport. There have been some serial offenders in the AFL. Notably one D. Brereton. Dermie has been retired for a few years now, but I certainly wouldn't risk getting under his skin. I reckon he'd still have the fire in the belly to do some damage if you pushed him. I only got suspended once and that was for whacking Hawthorn legend Michael Tuck. I didn't hurt him at all but it was Michael Tuck, so they gave me a week for hitting a great bloke.

> I've decided to start *rubbing out* the kids, instead of grounding them. And to make it easier for everyone, I'm bringing in a points system. Back chat? Two hours without the phone. Late home? Four hours without the computer. If you have a poor record, the penalty is worse. All clear? Good.

rubber: a condom.

Other slang names for a condom include: dinger, franger, raincoat, love glove, the goalie and party hat.

runner, to do a: to run away from a cab without paying.

I did it by accident once. I was so drunk I thought it was my mate who was driving me home. No wonder he didn't want to come in for another drink.

rust bucket: an old car.

The car can be covered in rust or it can just be an affectionate term for an old car. You could probably also use it to describe an old redheaded person. My first car was a rust bucket. My mate said he'd remove all the rust for me. When I went to pick up the car, all that was left was a steering wheel.

'S' is the letter on the front of Superman's outfit. He always had that outfit on underneath his normal clothes, which would make it a bit stinky. Hopefully, he had one outfit for each day, like you do with undies. Some blokes like to stretch that rule a bit. Superman can do anything unless there's kryptonite around. Kryptonite makes him useless and weak. How much fun could you have with him if you worked in his office? Stir a teaspoon of kryptonite in with his coffee. Bake some kryptonite cookies. Hide some kryptonite in the lining of his car door. Not sure where you'd get the kryptonite from, though. Probably Bunnings. They've got everything else. If some other place had a better price on kryptonite, Bunnings would beat it by 10 per cent.

Saab: luxurious Swedish car manufacturers.

Had some really different-looking models in their time. Known for safety features. Jerry Seinfeld drove one. Some models even had wipers on the headlights, because the last thing you want is for your headlights to not be able to see where they're going.

sack, get the: to have your job terminated.

It can happen if you constantly arrive late to work or if you stuff up all the time or if you're sleeping with the boss's wife. Don't expect to get a letter of recommendation either. Although, depending on how good you were, you might get one from the boss's wife.

safe as houses: couldn't be any safer.

Usually said by a person who has just built something that looks pretty dodgy and is bound to fall down any minute.

Saints: St Kilda Football Club.

The mighty Sainters! Have won only one premiership in their history, back in 1966. They got pretty close against the Cats in 2009 and even closer when they drew with the Pies in 2010, but luck hasn't really gone their way. Their supporters have been through a lot but continue to hang in there because they're as tough as nails and slightly crazy.

Salvos: the Salvation Army.

They help people in need and raise money through their op shops. You can often find a gem of a bargain in a

Salvo op shop. I saw some golf clubs that were just like mine but at one-tenth of their price. I quickly discovered that they were mine and the Darl had some explaining to do.

sandgroper: someone from Western Australia.
Named after a burrowing insect found in Western Australia. Not that impressive a nickname now, is it?

sanger: sandwich.
Can also be toasted, in which case it is called a 'toasted sanger'. Any number of things can be put in a sanger. I like your basic ham, cheese and tomato one, and I like it when you go to a function and they cut the sandwiches into those little triangles because it makes you feel like you're a giant with massive hands and a huge mouth. Then you burn your mouth with a cup of coffee and crawl off to the toilets with tears in your eyes.

sawn-off shotgun: a shotgun with the barrel sawn off.
It is shorter and easier to carry around, which is why it is often used in armed robberies. Why do some armed robbers wear clown masks? How are we supposed to take them seriously? Is that gun going to fire bullets or confetti?

scalper: someone who buys tickets for an event and then resells them at a much higher price.
The AFL made sure scalping was outlawed for the grand final, which is a really good thing. Unless, of course, your team is playing and you're desperate for a ticket, or you bought tickets thinking your team was going to play and they never made it. Even though scalping is banned, you still see people wandering around outside before the game, holding signs saying, 'Ticket wanted'. Are they expecting someone who has gone

to the trouble of buying a ticket and getting themselves to the game to suddenly decide *Hang on. You know what? I think I might sell this ticket to someone.*

scam: a dodgy business idea; to trick someone into handing over money.

There are heaps of scams on the internet. One of the most common involves a person from overseas who has inherited loads of money but needs your bank account to funnel the funds out of the country, of which you'll get a good share. You hand over your bank details and they clean out your account. By the third time it happened to me, I started to wise up.

scarper: to leave quickly.

Especially if you've done something wrong. I had to scarper the other day after I knocked over a stand of postcards at the newsagent's. I hope the guy they landed on is all right.

schnoz: nose.

A lot of blokes have copped one in the schnoz on the football field or in the pub. Some people have a big schnoz, some have a crooked schnoz, some have a red schnoz. I'm happy with my schnoz; it never gets any negative comments. Unfortunately, the rest of my features make up for it.

scoff: to eat quickly.

I tend to scoff and I think it just shows that I'm enjoying the food. I also don't like my food to get cold, so by scoffing, you're eating it while it's still warm. The key is to not make a mess when you're scoffing because then you just look like a greedy pig. I've perfected the art of non-messy scoffing, and I'm thinking of running some classes on it. It could be a nice little earner, and I'd get to scoff stuff while I'm demonstrating. It's a win/win for Billy.

scone: head; your noggin.

My scone got punched heaps on the
footy field, mainly from backmen,
who conveniently missed the ball but
connected with the back of my head.
The front of my head is still pretty
hard but the back of my head is like
a beanbag.

scorcher: a really hot day.

A great word to say too: 'It's a
real scorcher today!' I love saying it. Once I tried to pass off a
26-degree day as a scorcher, just so I would get
to say it. The guy at the fruit shop challenged me on it and
said, 'I don't think you can class a 26-degree day as a scorcher,
Billy.' I locked him in my boot. He wasn't going to spoil my day.

Scott no mates: someone with no mates.

You call someone 'Scott no mates' because it sounds like 'he's
got no mates'. If you see someone you know standing all alone
at any time, you might yell out, 'Hey, Scott! Scott no mates!' If
someone has done or said something that may have offended
people and resulted in him being disliked, then you can also
call him 'Scott'. What a shame. I always thought Scott was a
good name. It certainly doesn't deserve to be tarnished in this
fashion. I think the Scotts of the world should band together
and do something to change this. Then we'll really get to see
if Scotts have any mates.

screamer: a spectacular mark in footy.

Also known as a 'speckie'. I've been known to take a few in my
time. I don't feature much on any of the AFL's greatest marks
packages. In the few where I do make an appearance, Gary

Ablett is on my shoulders. Most of my great screamers must have been taken at games that weren't televised.

scrub up all right: you say this when someone looks good when they're dressed up.
Unfortunately, I hear this statement every time I wear a suit, which doesn't say much for my casual clothes. Then again, the last time I went shopping for new clothes was about fifteen years ago. Maybe I shouldn't bother spending my money. If I hold on to these clothes for another couple of years, they'll be back in fashion again.

scruffy: messy and untidy.
Shabbily dressed. Also known as 'the Billy look'.

scumbag: the lowest of the low; someone who is detested by everyone else.
Sometimes people's professions put them in this category. For example, parking inspectors, used-car salesmen, real-estate agents, journalists and ex-footballers still trying to cash in on a long gone career.

seafood diet: my favourite diet because it's very simple. See food and eat it.

see a man about a dog: to go somewhere.
Something you say when you have to leave without giving away the real reason you're leaving. Often said when you want to go to the toilet. Vets couldn't use it because it sounds like something they might really have to do. I'm going to take it upon myself to come up with a saying that vets can use in

its place. Okay. How about 'I have to go see a clown about a sawn-off shotgun.' Mmm, maybe they should stick with the original.

set of wheels: a car.

Often used when referring to someone buying a new car. Can apply to other vehicles as well. I'd probably draw the line at the smaller vehicles. I wouldn't class a shopping trolley as a set of wheels. Besides, it's never got the full set of wheels any-way. It's always three normal wheels and a wonky one. Also means new shoes (for blokes). As in, 'Nice set of wheels.'

settle down: take it easy; relax.

What you say to someone who is getting a bit hot under the collar. You're at a pub and someone starts to get a bit testy after a few too many frothies and a bloke has to step in and say, 'Settle down, mate.' I don't like being the bloke saying set-tle down because you're often the one who gets punched first. I'd much rather be the guy standing behind that bloke holding a bar stool.

seven-year itch: the stage of your marriage when you get bored and start looking for other partners.

It's supposed to be a common thing. I don't subscribe to it, of course. This is made easy by my inability to remember my wedding anniversary. It's a bit hard to have a 'seven-year itch' when you've got no idea how many years you've been married.

shagger's back: a sore back as a result of having too much sex.

Even a person who is incredibly shy, nervous and not likely to be in a relationship can walk into work with a sore back and everyone will suggest that person has shagger's back.

shattered: very upset; emotionally destroyed.
The feeling I get when I'm at a mate's place and he says he only has light beer in the fridge.

shell out: to pay money for.
When you've got kids, you're shelling out for heaps of stuff. Not a day goes by when I don't have to pay for something for my kids. It could be school-related, sports-related or just 'generally being a kid'-related. It's never ending. At least if you're shelling out heaps of cash on a car, you can sell it later and get some of your money back.

shellacking: a bad defeat; when you are totally smashed by the opposition.
Not good to be on the end of one of these. The Gold Coast Suns and Greater Western Sydney better get used to it in their early days and the journos better come up with another word for 'shellacking' because you can't use it every week.

shemozzle: a mess; disarray; something that is really disorganised.
I've been to heaps of bucks' nights that have been a shemozzle. Everyone puts in money to cover beer, food and a bus and you end up running out of beer, only getting one spring roll each, getting locked out of the bus and losing half the blokes along the way. You ring the buck about midnight on his mobile to see if he's okay. He's sober, sitting in Macca's, having a couple of cheeseburgers and wondering where everyone has gone.

shenanigans: up to no good; mucking around.

My hand is up. I have been involved in my fair share of shenanigans over the years and would like to take this opportunity to apologise to those people I have embarrassed, hurt or left financially worse off. You all know who you are, and I'm sorry. This apology in no way means that I will compensate you for any costs incurred or emotional trauma experienced.

shifty: dishonest; unable to be trusted.

A person or a deal can be shifty. Sometimes both at the same time. Most people have one member of their family who is a bit shifty. They're often the ones who organise a group present for another relative. They collect all the money from everyone and then spend less on the actual present. Collecting money and then buying a present is a pain in the arse, so if the same person is volunteering to do it every time, then there's reason to be suspicious.

shiner: a black eye.

A symbol of courage or your inability to handle yourself in a fight. I'd be going with the first one if I were you.

shithouse: no good.

Can apply to anything and everything. That movie was shithouse. That meal was shithouse. The service was shithouse. The décor was shithouse. The car ride into the city to go to the restaurant before the movie was shithouse. Overall, the night out was shithouse. For a first date, that'd be pretty shithouse.

shitkicker: someone who does the simple, boring and basic work in a business.

Some people start off as a shitkicker with the aim of working their way up. By doing this for a few years and impressing the right people, you never know, you could be promoted to 'Head Shitkicker'.

shit-scared: very scared.

You can't get more scared than shit-scared. As bad as it sounds, it can also be a bit of an adrenaline rush. I was shit-scared on a couple of the rides when we went to the Gold Coast. I wish one of them wasn't the bus ride to the theme parks.

shit-stirrer: someone who constantly makes fun of other people.

They like to cause trouble and offend others for their own enjoyment. Every workplace has its own shit-stirrer. He usually gets away with pushing people's buttons all year until someone punches him in the face at the Christmas party, to a round of applause.

shocker: particularly bad.

If you don't get a kick in a game of footy, you're said to have had a shocker. A bad joke could be a shocker. Here are some examples:

- What do you call a cow with no legs? Ground beef.
- Where does a general keep his army? Up his sleevy.
- What's brown and sticky? A stick.
- Did you hear about the circus fire? It was intense.
- What has four wheels and flies? A garbage truck.

I did warn you that they were shockers.

shonky: dodgy; crooked.

A person or a business can be shonky. The word 'shonky' is

often associated with second-hand-car dealerships. You can tell a shonky salesman by how hard he tries to get into your head to control your thinking. You need to make sure that you deflect all of his attempts. Never feel pressured into doing anything. You're your own person and you make your own decisions in your own time. Always remember, he's more desperate to sell than you are to buy. Of course, that's easier said than done. What if you really want that car, you haven't seen many in that condition, it comes with a good warranty, has only had one owner and you don't want to risk missing out on it? See, how it's turned around now? Because that's just me talking like a shonky salesman. Don't fall for it!

shot glass: a tiny glass you drink alcohol from.

A group of friends will be at a bar and at some stage during the night, usually when everybody is smashed, someone will buy a round of shots. In unison, everyone in the group throws the highly concentrated alcoholic drink straight down their throats. The thing about shots is that it's okay to give them crazy names. The crazier the name, the more people want to try it. Here are some popular shots that you can get: orgasm, slippery nipple, sex on the beach, granny punch, brain haemorrhage and gorilla fart. Coincidentally, three of those were also the nicknames of ex-teammates of mine.

shotgun wedding: a quickly organised wedding because the bride is pregnant.

People don't feel as much pressure today to get married if they're having a baby. A lot of people wait to have the baby and then when that baby becomes a toddler, they put it in the bridal party and get married. I've been to weddings where the guests spend the whole time speculating as to whether or not it's a shotgun wedding, until someone gets drunk enough to actually ask the bride. This usually results in an all-in brawl. As they say, it must have been a good wedding – the bride was in tears, the groom was in tears, even the cake was in tiers.

shout: a round of drinks.

When at the pub with your mates, you get into a shout with them and you have to follow the very strict rules that go along with it. You must join the shout. Don't even think about not being a part of it. Just buying drinks for yourself at your own pace is a big no-no. You cannot under any circumstances leave before you've shouted the group. You wouldn't make it to your car anyway. Don't wait to be told when it's your shout. It's a bad look. Anticipate it and have the drinks ready to go before they've finished their last glass. That's it. Pretty simple. Now off you go and don't stuff it up.

shut up shop: to close down; finish.

When a business goes broke, they often have to shut up shop. When your partner decides you're not getting any until you have the snip, then she's shut up shop.

sickie: a day off.

You don't necessarily have to be sick to take a sickie; you just need to have something better to do. In a lot of cases you're hung-over from the night before and have no choice but to take a sickie. More recently they've highlighted just how much money sickies have cost the economy. It still hasn't changed our behaviour and it never will.

silent but deadly: the breaking of wind without sound but still with smell.

The advantage being that if there is no noise coming from

your direction, then you can blame someone else. If there are only two of you in the room, that's a bit harder to do. If you're convincing enough you can eventually make someone else believe that they actually did it.

skinful: to have had enough of something.

If someone is drunk, then they've had a skinful. If they're drunk and really annoying you, then you've had a skinful.

skol: to drink a whole glass at once.

Skolling games are very popular and there are heaps of them around. 'Skol, skol, skol!' is often yelled out by the crowd in encouragement. Personally, I like to enjoy my beer, so I drink it slowly. Not too slowly though. You don't want it getting warm, otherwise it goes from beer to some weird alien fluid that is completely undrinkable.

sleazebag: a slimey, creepy bloke who tries to pick up chicks.

He usually directs his attention to chicks a lot younger than him. Chicks then start warning each other and he becomes a marked man. This doesn't put him off, though. He'll be back next time as sleazy as ever, so you've got to give him credit for persisting.

slob: an untidy, lazy bloke.

Probably covers 80 per cent of blokes. Me included. I pride myself on my slobbiness. It's taken me years to perfect. My aim is to get 100 per cent of blokes to be slobs. That way it will just be accepted as something all blokes do and we won't be given any grief for it. If you're not a slob then come and join us. It's for a good cause. We'll all be better off.

sloshed: drunk.

smashed: drunk.

snot rag: handkerchief.
The straightforward honesty of this name makes me laugh. Yes, it is a rag and yes, you keep your snot in it, so let's call it that.

sozzled: drunk.

sparkie: an electrician.
One of the more dangerous trades. If you come in contact with electricity you can die, basically. Now when they give you an astronomical bill for changing a light globe, you'll remember that they're risking their life so that you can see at night.

sparrow fart: very early in the morning; dawn.
Usually refers to the time someone got up: 'Woke up at sparrow fart.' I wonder if sparrows can do silent but deadly ones?

spew: to vomit; to chuck.
Not always bad. You can have a good spew. 'Yeah, I had a good spew and I feel so much better.' Even if you haven't eaten carrots for a year, they always turn up. Spew can also mean to be upset at something that didn't go your way. 'I was spewing we lost that game, so let's get drunk so that I can spew some more.'

split the difference: to find middle ground.
If someone wanted $12 500 for their car and you wanted to pay $12 300, you could split the difference and agree to pay $12 400. Some of the best deals ever made have been finalised with the phrase 'let's split the difference'. Some of the worst deals ever made have been finalised with that phrase too. If you're not quick enough to work out what the split of the

difference is, then you could get ripped off. It doesn't sound good to say, 'Okay, let's split the difference and it's a deal. Now, if you could just tell me what the difference is, we can sign off on this.'

spot-on: exactly; getting something right.

You could be hanging a picture and trying to get it straight. When you have lined it up correctly, your mate who is helping will say, 'Spot-on!' You can also say 'spot-on' when you're agreeing with a point being made by someone else: 'You know how you said beer is the best thing ever invented? You're spot-on.'

sprung: caught doing something you shouldn't have been doing.

It's not a lot of fun when you get sprung, but catching someone else doing the wrong thing is great fun because you get to yell out, 'Sprung!' If you say it loud enough, people come running from everywhere to see what is going on. This embarrasses the person even more.

square up: to get one back.

If someone whacks you in a game of footy, you can square up by getting them back later. I got whacked a fair bit, but every time I went to square up I got whacked even harder. In the end I'd just arrange for a teammate to square up on my behalf. As the unconscious bloke was being carried off on a stretcher, I'd always get in his face and say, 'You mess with me and I'll get you back . . . Okay, maybe I won't, but I'll find someone who will.'

squib: someone who doesn't go in hard for the ball; a coward.

Some guys can go through their whole career being a squib and get away with it. It's a real art making it look like you're not squibbing it. It's all about timing your run so that you get there a bit late for the contest . . . or so someone told me. How would I know that?

stack: to crash.
When you were young you'd stack your bike. When you got older you'd stack your car. It was a lot funnier and cheaper when you'd stack your bike.

stacks on: an exhortation to pile on top of each other.
If one person falls over, the closest person to them will yell, 'Stacks on!' before diving on top of them. Upon hearing 'Stacks on!' everyone runs over and dives onto the pile of bodies. Can be pretty dangerous, especially for the people on the bottom of the pile. They can struggle for air and/or get crushed, but, hey, don't let that spoil your fun.

stiff: unlucky.
You'd have to be pretty stiff to do your knee on the footy field, but not as stiff as you'd be if you did it while running through the banner. Teams have been stiff in some of our great games. They perhaps should've won, but that's the nature of footy. Some would say the Saints were stiff in the drawn 2010 Grand Final. Some would say a bad bounce of the ball cost them a premiership. Those people tend to forget that the ball bounced hundreds of times in all sorts of directions throughout the whole game.

stitch: a pain in your side during exercise.
The pissiest-sounding excuse you can use to get out of training. I've actually also used it to get out of doing other stuff. 'Billy, I thought you were going to mow the lawns?' 'I can't, I've got a stitch.'

stone's throw: not very far; a short distance.

We do tend to stretch the meaning as far as we can. Somewhere that is a kilometre away is still considered a stone's throw. That's either one light stone or one very strong wind.

streaker: a naked ground-invader.

Streaking used to happen regularly but then sporting bodies introduced fines and started putting a cap on the amount of alcohol you could buy in the stadium at one time. Streakers slowly disappeared and have joined the likes of the Tasmanian Tiger by becoming extinct. I miss them. The best part was the chase. There was nothing funnier than watching a streaker burst onto the ground and then spend the next five minutes evading the two fat cops who were chasing him. He would eventually slip over or get stopped by a player and then the cops would escort him off the ground while holding one of their hats over his private parts. If I was a cop, I wouldn't want to put any hat back on that's had someone else's wobbly bits dangling in it. You may as well put their undies on your head.

stubby: a small bottle of beer that is easy to hold and drink.

They come in a handy sixpack and/or a box of 24. Taking a sixpack to a party is pretty standard, even if you only plan on drinking a couple. You have to find the spot where the drinks are being kept cool (it could be an esky, the laundry sink or the bath), and you carefully place your stubbies in the ice. That's when the drama begins. You have to keep a keen eye on your stubbies because they can go missing. Some other bloke brings crap beer and then tries to drink yours all night. Sometimes I'd bring spare ones, having superglued the caps on. I'd mark them so that I wouldn't grab them and then just watch that stubby-stealer rip the skin from his hand trying to twist off the top.

stubby holder: a foam, rubber (or some other material) cover for a stubby.

It keeps the stubby cool on the inside and your hand doesn't get cold. Personally, I'm not a big fan of the stubby holder. I like to hold the stubby directly, without a barrier between us. I like to feel it. Using a stubby holder is like wearing a condom during sex.

stud: a bloke who gets a bit of action with the ladies.

Some blokes go through periods where they are studs and then will inexplicably have a quiet patch, only to find form again later. At some point in your life, though, your ability to be a stud diminishes. It's not an easy thing to come to terms with, which is why a lot of blokes continue to tell stories about what a stud they are long after they've seen any action.

Before you decide you're a *stud*, check out creep (page 33), octopus (page 146) and sleazebag (page 201).

stuffed: ruined; broken; wrecked.

Often yelled out in frustration when you real-ise that your efforts to fix something are a waste of time. 'It's stuffed!' Stuffed also means to be tired. 'I'm stuffed!' For most of my career I was stuffed after running out onto the ground. I can't believe that these days they come out onto the ground for a full-on warm up as well. If they had asked me to do that, I would have told them to get stuffed!

stumps: the end.

Traditionally, it's the end of the day's play in cricket, but it also means to stay until the end of a party or drinking session.

If you've been out with mates and were one of the last to leave, and the next day someone asks what time you left, you say, 'I was there till stumps.' It's a pretty good achievement – just like batting in cricket till stumps, except you get a hangover with this one.

succinct: concise, clear.
This is a very handy word. Whenever someone is going into way too much detail about something, just ask them to succinct it for you.

sucked in: to be tricked or deceived.
If being tricked isn't embarrassing enough, having a group of people pointing, laughing and all saying, 'Sucked in!' is enough to make you want to crawl into a hole. April Fool's Day is when everyone tries to suck each other in. You should be on your toes that of all days. No excuses for being sucked in on 1 April. Except for the year 2017, of course, when there is no 1 April due to that calendar hiccup we go through once every 600 years. The first of April is removed to make up for the extra couple of seconds that are added to the last day of every year. That's how it originally became April Fool's Day.

Paulie calls Tony Soprano 'T' in *The Sopranos*, which I reckon is a pretty cool nickname. Sure, T orders the execution of people but you still somehow barrack for him. There is Mr T, of course, who played a badass boxer called 'Clubber Lang' in *Rocky III* in 1982 before going on to star as B.A. Baracus in *The A Team*. His tough-guy image went back a lot further than that. He used to be a bouncer and then a bodyguard for some of America's richest people, including Diana Ross. His real name is Laurence Tureaud. He's the youngest of twelve children and grew up in a housing project in Chicago. That would've toughened him up. He is well known for his gold chains and rings. Not many people could get away with wearing that much jewellery and not have fun made of them.

tab: the bill.

You can have your own tab at a pub and pay it off at a later stage. My favourite five words to hear someone else say are, 'I'll pick up the tab.' You should see their faces when they get the bill and realise how much I've been drinking. There's also the other tab. The one you go to when you want to bet. It's in capital letters: TAB. It stands for Totalisator Agency Board, which is how I like to say it. That way people don't know you're just going somewhere to bet. It actually sounds like you're going somewhere important. I'll say, 'I've just got to go to the Totalisator Agency Board.' Everyone else is sitting there, thinking to themselves, *Wow, Billy's going to be making some high-powered decisions at some special board meeting.* They're partly right. I'll certainly be making some high-powered decisions but just on which horses I should put in my quaddie.

tag: to pull the tag off someone's jeans.

You have to be quick, so the jeans wearer won't be able to do anything about it. Always fun, until you pull a chunk of the jeans off with the tag.

tag dag: someone whose tag or label is sticking out the top of their shirt or jacket.

You can either go over and tuck it back in for them without drawing other people's attention to it, or you can just sit back in your chair and yell, 'Tag dag!' I'd be more inclined to go with the lazier option.

tailgate: driving right up the bum of the car in front of you.

A completely unnecessary and dangerous thing to do. We still do it, though, because we can't stand it when someone drives so slow they may as well be walking! On the other hand, we also hate it when someone tailgates us. A common response is to brake suddenly. Yeah, having the back of your own car smashed in, that'll teach them.

take a load off: to sit down and put your feet up.
I probably take a load off a bit too often, even when I don't need to. I might start taking a load on every now and again just to get the balance right.

take a walk: move on; get out of here.
Often said to someone who is causing trouble. I like saying it to those annoying people who approach you to do a survey in shopping centres. 'Take a walk, buddy, and don't look back.'

take the piss: to laugh at someone's expense; to poke fun at a person.
Even if you say something that they may find hurtful and offensive, you can always give yourself an out by saying, 'Come on, mate. I was just taking the piss.' Then it's up to him whether or not he wants to deck you.

takeaway: fast food.
One of my favourite cuisines. Yes, I count it as a cuisine. Not sure how I'd survive without takeaway. Friday-night fish 'n' chips are part of the staple diet for most Australians. Throw in some pizza, Macca's, Subway, KFC, noodles and Indian and you've got every day of the week covered. If you cook stuff in the kitchen and take it away to the dining room to eat, then it's not much different to driving up the road to the Thai place and bringing it back to the dining room. Okay, maybe we should cook at home one night of the week. There you go, I'm prepared to make a concession.

talk shop: to talk about work when you're not at work.
People often do this at parties or bars. It's really annoying when two people do this and you're standing next to them. I just ask them what their boss's name is and when they tell me, I say they're a friend of mine. They shut up about work pretty quickly after that.

tank: to lose a game of footy on purpose.
Teams have been accused of doing this so that they'll get good draft picks. The teams, of course, deny this is the case. Let's hope the draft picks flourish as expected or they may have to tank again.

technicolour yawn: spew; vomit.
A clever description, I reckon, although you might not see the humour in it when you're leaning over the dunny, spewing your guts out.

thick ear, I'll give you a: to give someone a whack to the head.
More often than not you were threatened with getting a thick ear rather than actually receiving one. I wish someone had told the fathers in those days to alternate the ears when giving out these. I've got a mate whose left ear is now twice the size of his right one.

thick skin, to have a: to be able to handle criticism or taunting.
You need to have a thick skin playing footy because of the abuse you cop from over the fence. The fact that a lot of the abuse is difficult to understand or just doesn't make sense helps you deal with it. I was forever asking supporters to submit their abuse in writing so that I could try to work out what they meant by it.

think tank: a meeting where people throw ideas around, work-related.

Also called a 'brainstorm session'. Someone writes down everything that is said and puts it on a whiteboard, then two weeks later it's all forgotten about. It was as if the think tank never happened. The term 'think tank' is one of those well-known business phrases that sits in the same basket as 'Let's do lunch', 'I'll get my people to call your people' and 'I didn't break the pho-
tocopier. It was like that when I found it, I swear'.

thirsty work: hard work.

Work that makes you want to have a drink, especially beer, afterwards. So, a lot of things qualify as thirsty work for me. Mowing the lawn – thirsty work. Going to the tip – thirsty work. Emptying the dishwasher – thirsty work. Watching TV – thirsty work.

three on the tree: a manual car with three gears on a column shift.

It's not often you hop into a car these days and get to say, 'Three on the tree!' Most of the more recent manual cars have got at least four or five forward gears and reverse, of course. I drove my brother's old car and found three on the tree really difficult until he told me that it was four on the floor and that I'd stuffed his indicator stick.

thrown together: a standard chick response to a compliment about their outfit.

'Oh, it's just something I've thrown together.' They never tell you they spent three hours in front of the mirror 'throwing it together'.

thumping: a bad beating.

It could be an individual beating, as in, 'He copped a thumping for opening his big mouth'. Or it could be a group thing, as in, 'Their team copped a thumping from the other side'. It can also be used to refer to a massive kick, as in, 'That was a thumping kick from Billy Brownless. It must've gone 70 metres!'

ticker: the heart.

In sport, if someone shows a lot of commitment, determination and guts, you would say that person has a big ticker. I have never been known for the size of my ticker, but I have for the size of my appetite.

*All the Good Blokes in this book have **ticker**. Just look for the symbol.*

tickets on himself: someone who thinks he's pretty good and is a bit of a head case.

I love bringing these people down to earth by going up to them and taking the imaginary tickets off them. Sure, they think you're weird initially, but they eventually appreciate you pointing out that they've been giving everyone the shits.

Tigers: Richmond Football Club.

It hasn't had the best couple of decades but has the best theme song, and a strong and loyal supporter base that will see them get through the hard times and be around to experience the success when it finally comes. I was there when the Cats came good, and, trust me, it's worth the wait.

tight-arse: someone who doesn't like spending money, often at the expense of others.

We've all got a mate who's a tight-arse and he can drive you mad because he's constantly trying to get out of paying for stuff. If you're at a bar, he's the last to go for his wallet when the beers are ordered; when you're having a dinner, he won't split the bill evenly and will only pay for exactly what he had, despite drinking all the wine that everyone else brought along. If he doesn't want or use something he owns, he'll never just give it to you; he'll make you pay for it and if you have given him something of yours to keep, he'll sell it on eBay when he's had enough of it and keep the profits. It's good to want to save money and not spend it willy-nilly but don't do it to the point where you're ripping off your own mates. If your tight-arse mate wants to borrow this book, do yourself and me a favour and suggest that he buys one himself. Or sell him yours and we'll split the profits.

time bomb: something or someone that could go off any minute.

It could be a situation or a person. A variant is a 'ticking time bomb'. If a person is feeling the pressure, either applied by others or just from the circumstances they find themselves in, then they could be a time bomb just waiting to explode. That's when you need a bomb-disposal unit for people. You ring them up and they come to diffuse the person. I'm not sure whether they'd need to cut a blue or red wire, but they would probably still need to wear the protective gear.

tin arse: someone who is lucky.

Often involves them winning money or always landing on their feet. I'd be happy to be a tin arse for just one day at the races. I'd even take being a tin arse only for one race. As long as I knew which race it was beforehand so that I could really load up.

tinny: a can of beer.
Nothing excites me more than walking out of a bottle shop carrying a slab of VB cans. You get to your car and strap them in like you did with your kids the first time you brought them home from hospital.

tip: a place to dump your rubbish.
As a kid, whenever Dad said that we were going to the tip, you'd get a similar feeling in your tummy to the one you used to get at Easter and Christmas time. As you were driving there, you'd dream that maybe this time you'd see a bike in good condition sticking out of the rubbish like a beacon. You'd then be able to take that bike home, fix it up, put a new seat on it, maybe give it a paint job and then raise it as your very own. You'd be the envy of the town on your reconditioned super-bike. Then one day I saw a front wheel and handlebars sticking out of the rubbish, so I rushed over and pulled it out, only to discover that it was just that – a front wheel and handlebars.

tipsy: a little bit drunk.

tits: boobs.

titties: boobs.
Rhyming slang: Salt Lake Cities.

toast: the raising and then drinking of alcohol when honouring someone.
Often done to the bride and groom and the bridesmaids at a wedding. The job of the person proposing the toast is one of the easiest official duties ever. It basically goes like this: 'I would like to propose a toast to the bridesmaids. To the bridesmaids!' Then everyone else yells out, 'To the bridesmaids!' Then people sit down. Sure, sometimes there's a bit to do beforehand,

like saying, 'A bit of shush please . . . could we have a bit of shush? . . . Come on, everyone, a bit of shush! . . . Hey! How about everyone SHUT THE F#*K UP!'

toasted sanger: a heated-up sandwich.

What a bloke will often try to pass off as a meal when he's left to cook for the family.

toey: eager to do something; very keen.

How you feel before a game of footy. A feeling usually long gone by quarter-time, especially if you're being given a good touch up.

ton: 100 runs in cricket.

I have a few to my name. All in backyard cricket. A lot easier to make runs when your younger brother is bowling and doing all the fielding, and he can't find the ball in a bush.

tonguey: sticking your tongue in when you kiss.

It really can get things going, providing you haven't been going at it for five minutes before realising your tongue is in her nostril instead of her mouth.

tonk: to smash the ball in cricket.

When you need to score runs fast. Unfortunately, when I played cricket I'd see any situation as a good opportunity to go the tonk. We'd only need three runs to win off five overs with nine wickets down and the batsman at the non-striker's end is on 99 – yep, looks like as good a time as any for Billy to go the tonk!

tool: an idiot.

An annoying bloke who rubs people up the wrong way. What your mate might call you if you do something stupid. I can't remember when I was last called one. I really need to spend more time with my mates.

⭐ **toolies: older blokes who head to the Gold Coast during schoolies week so that they can pick up drunk younger girls.**

They're regarded as desperate and incapable of having a relationship with a woman their own age. Schoolies can spot toolies a mile away. They look older and wear clothes that were in fashion ten years ago.

top dog: the person in charge, officially or unofficially.

It could be at a workplace. It could be at a prison. Sometimes it is obvious who the top dog is, other times you need to ask. I'm pretty sure Ronald McDonald is the top dog at Macca's, but the kid I asked behind the counter wasn't sure.

top shelf: the best of its type.

Often used to refer to alcohol. It mightn't actually be the best, but someone will try to convince you that it's the best by claiming it as top shelf. By the fifth drink you don't really care anyway.

tosser: a wanker.

A bloke who likes to crap on about how good he is and how much he knows about stuff. Sometimes they are confined to a particular area of expertise. One bloke could be a wine tosser. He's the type who sticks his nose in the glass and swishes the wine around in his mouth before drinking it. It's wine! It's pretty simple. People grow grapes, then squash the grapes, and we drink the juice. That's what wine is. Sure, I like a good wine more than the really cheap stuff and prefer a full-bodied red, especially if it's a shiraz from Heathcote, because the soil there is perfectly suited for that type of grape. That reminds me, I need to arrange the bottles in my cellar in order of vintage.

totalled: a car wrecked beyond repair.

If you crash your car, it always makes for a better story when you say it was totalled. If you can drive your car home after a crash, it's hard to impress anyone when telling them about the accident.

⭐ totes: an abbreviation of the word 'totally'.

It is usually followed by the word 'epic' to describe an event or action that is either very enjoyable or intense and crazy: 'That party was totes epic, babe!' I can't believe I had to just write that.

touch wood: a saying to protect yourself from bad luck.

A thing superstitious people say after they've just mentioned something good that has happened. Some people like to actually touch wood when they say it. Problem is, it's really hard to find something made out of wood these days. I was with a friend in his car when he said, 'Touch wood.' He pulled over and then went into a café just to touch the wooden table. I ordered a coffee so that we wouldn't look rude.

tracky-dacks: tracksuit pants.

The most comfortable item of clothing we own. So comfortable in fact that we'll wear them down the shops and not care that we look a bit shabby. A very versatile pant. Can also be worn while watching telly, mowing the lawn, at the TAB, at the footy, at the movies or at any birthday drinks where the dress code has not been specified. Holes in your tracky-dacks aren't frowned upon, they just add character. So do paint stains. Tracky-dacks should be made part of the official Australian National Costume along with the Bonds singlet and the full-sleeve tattoo. Tracky-dacks are the hardest item of clothing to chuck out when their time has come. You become very attached to them and they constantly remind you of the good times you had together. It's okay to shed a tear when the missus yanks them out of your hands and puts them into the big plastic bag of stuff to go to the tip.

⭐ **tramp stamp: a tattoo on the lower part of a girl's back, just above her bum.**   · TEENAGE SPEAK ·

It became very common in the '90s and this trend somehow led to the girls being labelled as common and promiscuous. People jokingly say that in 50 years' time it will be known as the 'gramp stamp'.

trots: harness racing.

Not as popular as it used to be in Australia. The horses race at a trotting pace and pull a driver in a two-wheeled cart called a sulkie. I usually have a bit of a sulkie when my horse doesn't win. The trots can also mean regularly running to the toilet because of diarrhoea. If a friend wants to take you to see the trots, before you say yes, make sure they're talking about the one with the horses.

tucker: food.

If we like the food, we'll say it's 'good tucker'. Recently I was with a mate who was getting stuck into the food and he said, 'Good tucker.' To which I replied, 'Just hurry up so we can get

out of here. We didn't even know the guy whose wake it is.'

🌸 **Tupperware party: a party that chicks have where they sell plastic containers.**

Don't be fooled. This is just another excuse to have a gathering where they can drink wine. How many plastic containers do they need, anyway? When is enough enough? What they really need to be selling is a big plastic container to keep all of the plastic containers in.

turd: excrement.

Often used to refer to someone who isn't a very nice person. Also Irish for 'third'.

turn it up: an expression used when you're not happy with what someone has done or said.

Probably the politest way you can tell someone that you're pissed off with them.

turps: alcohol.

'U' means 'you' in text and computer speak. We've become too lazy or just no longer have time to write the whole word. I ask you: Are we ruining the English language? I'm genuinely concerned and this is coming from a bloke who has butchered the English language heaps of times – by accident, of course. If I'm worried, then I think we all should be. Something deep down inside me wants to protect our great language before it's too late. U with me?

UFO: unidentified flying object; an alien spaceship.
There are sightings all the time but as of yet we have not
had any proof that a spacecraft from another planet has
landed on earth or even entered our atmosphere. Most
reported sightings can be explained as aircraft, balloons,
meteors or bright planets. There are also heaps of hoaxes,
which do a great job of wasting everyone's time. That still
leaves a few sightings that can't be explained. They certainly fit under the category of UFO. I
personally believe that if aliens
had the ability to come here,
they'd stop, get out and have a
look around. If we went for a
drive somewhere we hadn't been
before, we'd get out of the car and
check it out. Even if the aliens weren't
sure where they were, you'd think they'd
get out and ask for directions.

Umpires' weapon of
torture — the whistle. Once the
whistle is blown the crowd usually fires
abuse at the man in white for having
a pea brain (see page 159).
Or something along those lines.

**umpire: bloke in white (or red,
yellow and green these days) who
runs around on the footy field
blowing his whistle.**
It's a tough job they do and I wouldn't
want it. It's much more fun being on the
other side of the fence yelling stuff at them.

under the influence: drunk.

under the pump: to be under a lot of pressure.
You could be under the pump at work or in a game of footy
or desperately trying to find coins in your car in the drive-
thru at Macca's with five cars banked up behind you.

under the thumb: to be under someone else's control.

Usually applied to a bloke and his wife. If a bloke says he can't come somewhere or has to go home early, the first conclusion we jump to is that he's under the thumb. Why? Because we all are and know exactly what he's going through.

under wraps: to keep something hidden for a while.

One of the best 'under wraps' stories has to be the winged keel on *Australia II*. We won the America's Cup in 1983 after it'd been held by the New York

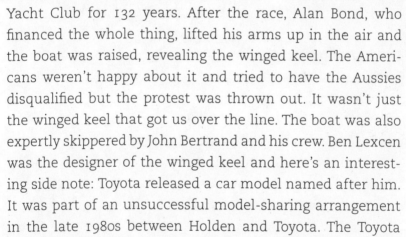

Yacht Club for 132 years. After the race, Alan Bond, who financed the whole thing, lifted his arms up in the air and the boat was raised, revealing the winged keel. The Americans weren't happy about it and tried to have the Aussies disqualified but the protest was thrown out. It wasn't just the winged keel that got us over the line. The boat was also expertly skippered by John Bertrand and his crew. Ben Lexcen was the designer of the winged keel and here's an interesting side note: Toyota released a car model named after him. It was part of an unsuccessful model-sharing arrangement in the late 1980s between Holden and Toyota. The Toyota Lexcen was in fact a VN Holden Commodore in disguise. We Aussies know our cars and you can't try to pass off a Commodore as another car by changing the front grille and a couple of badges. How stupid do they think we are?

225

undies: underpants.

They come in all shapes and sizes and colours. We blokes usually own about seven pairs of them and they all seem to pack it in around about the same time. Some blokes prefer the brief undies, while others prefer the trunks. Most of the time their wives buy their new undies, so they have no choice in the matter anyway.

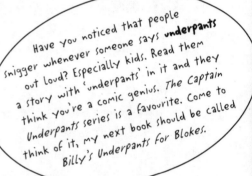

up shit creek without a paddle: in a bit of trouble.

I also wouldn't recommend fishing in shit creek either.

Have you noticed that people snigger whenever someone says **underpants** out loud? Especially kids. Read them a story with 'underpants' in it and they think you're a comic genius. The Captain Underpants series is a favourite. Come to think of it, my next book should be called Billy's Underpants for Blokes.

up yours: get stuffed

Often used when addressing umpires.

useless as: not useful at all.

Often followed by one of these:

    an ashtray on a motorbike

    a fart in a colander

    tits on a tomcat

    a chocolate teapot

    a screen door on a submarine

U-turn: turning your car around to go in the opposite direction.

A dangerous thing to attempt if not done carefully. Has caused heaps of accidents. Also known as a U-ie. Sometimes you see a road sign that says 'no U-turn' and it's usually in a spot where you want to do one and where you'd imagine a lot of other people wanting to do one as well. Why do they always put the sign at that spot?

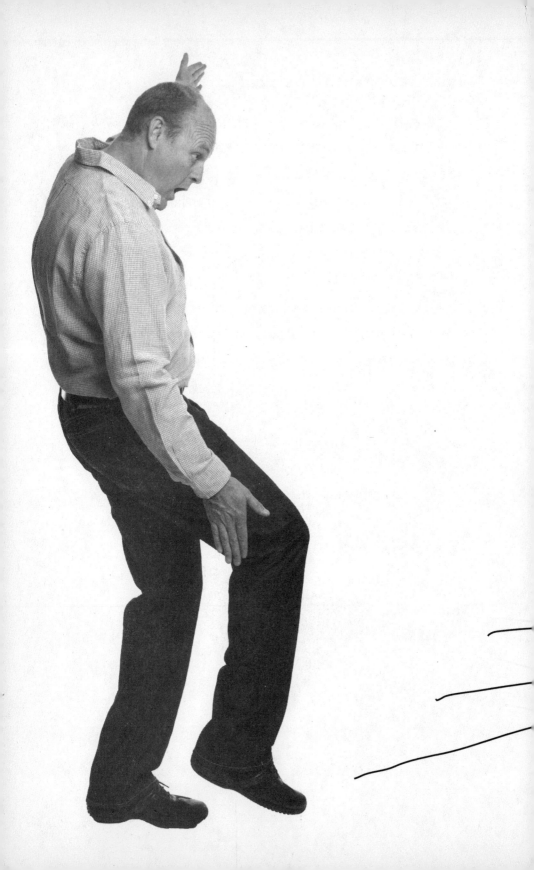

V is an energy drink. I reckon the whole energy drink thing is way out of control. There were no energy drinks when I was growing up and we survived pretty well without them. No one was falling asleep or feeling too tired to perform at work or school. Having said that, I like the taste of V more than any of them. When I think of 'V' though, I think of the Big V. The Big V would have to be one of the best-looking footy jumpers around. It just looks so powerful and intimidating. I remember watching those interstate games when I was young and they were awesome. Unfortunately, with the expansion of the AFL, the interstate rivalry got lost. I get jealous when I see how big it is in the NRL State of Origin series. That's the only thing about the NRL that I do get jealous about, by the way.

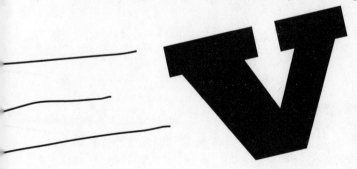

Van Deimen's Land: the original name of Tasmania.

Better not leave Tassie out. They love their footy and might have a team of their own one day.

VB: Australia's (and Billy's) favourite beer.

VCR: video home system; video cassette recorder.

An invention that revolutionised how we watched television in the late '70s–early '80s. You could tape shows and play them back later. You could also rent movies and watch them in your very own home. The dilemma at the time was which format to go with. Beta was considered to be better quality but everyone was buying VHS. In the end VHS won the battle in Australia and those who bought a Beta found themselves forking out for a VHS player a few years later. Have you tried watching anything on video now that we have DVD? Looks pretty crap.

'Happy Little **Vegemites**' is a line from the 1950s ad that came to apply to any group of contented people. I was a happy little Vegemite when the Cats won premierships in 2007 and 2009.

Vegemite: a dark-coloured spread to put on bread.

An Aussie icon. Everyone's got a photo of them as a kid with a Vegemite moustache. It is made from yeast extract and is a by-product of beer manufacturing. See, even the stuff left over from making beer we shove down our throats.

verbal diarrhoea: talk coming out of someone's mouth that's just a constant flow of boring and useless drivel.

There's nothing worse than when you get cornered at a party and have to listen to this. Unlike normal diarrhoea, you can't flush this to make it go away.

village idiot: a person regarded as the biggest fool at a particular place.

They're considered to be the number-one idiot. For example, Shane Crawford on *The Footy Show*.

VIP: very important person.

A lot of bars have a designated area for VIPs, which, by the end of the night, stands for 'Very Intoxicated Person'.

VW: Volkswagen; German car company that made the beetle and the kombi van.

Volkswagen means 'people's car' in German. Hitler wanted a car that ordinary German families could afford so in 1934 he commissioned Ferdinand Porsche (yes, that Porsche) to develop the Volkswagen beetle. I really like the way the new beetle has incorporated the look of the original beetle. Still nowhere near as good as a Ford, though.

'W' is the middle initial in George Bush's name. It stands for Walker; I didn't even know that was a name. Anyway, it didn't stop him becoming president. The W-class tram is the old-looking tram that Melbourne is famous for. The first one was made in 1923. We gave one to Denmark as a present when Princess Mary and Prince Frederik had their first kid. Not sure what we expected them to do with a tram. I think they've dismantled it and used the parts to make a billy cart for the young prince.

WAGs: the wives and girlfriends of sportsmen.

Some of them go on to become a bigger name than their partners. They really come into their own when there's a big night like the Brownlow medal. They dress up and strut their stuff on the red carpet. If the Hollywood tape doesn't do its job, then the outfits can end up being more revealing than the wags intended.

wanker: a bloke who talks absolute rubbish and thinks he's pretty cool.

You can be a wanker just through your actions as well. There are plenty of them out there, let me tell you. A lot of them drive a specific model of car because they think it makes them look better than everyone else. They'll only wear certain clothes and hang out in certain bars and restaurants. If any wankers out there could send in the names of these bars and restaurants, then the rest of us normal people could avoid them.

Warnie: the world's best spinner.

Good BLOKE

watering hole: a favourite place to drink at; the pub you always go to.

If you happen to be their favourite patron, then there's really something special you've got going there.

wedgie: the pulling up of a bloke's undies so that they wedge in his crack.

A great Australian pastime that we all learn to do as kids and have perfected by the time we're adults. Sure, it's pretty juvenile but the best jokes are.

well-hung: a bloke who's pretty big in the downstairs department.

You know you are when you walk out of the showers and your teammates give you a standing ovation.

wheelie: a move where you're riding one-wheeled on a bicycle or motorbike.

It's normally the back wheel. If you can do it on the front wheel then that is super-impressive. I once did it on my bike and the front wheel must've been loose because it just flew off. I had nothing to land on, so I had to ride all the way home doing a wheelie. It was going well until I had to turn a corner. With the wheel you turn on not being there, the handlebars become useless. Fortunately, there was a parked car that I could bring my front forks down on. Unfortunately, there was a guy sitting in that car. Hopefully, the bike I left him when I ran off makes up for the damage I caused to his boot.

wheelie bin: something that has to be put outside once a week.

This is a bloke's job. The hardest part is remembering to do it before you're told to. A good clue that it's bin night is when you see the neighbours' bins out on the street. Go straight inside and wheel yours out.

whinger: someone who complains about stuff all the time.

There's usually one person at work who just whinges all day. You're there listening and thinking to yourself, *If you hate it so much here then why don't you go and get a job somewhere else? Preferably somewhere far enough away from me so that I can't hear you whinging any more.*

William Shakespeare: regarded as one of the greatest writers of all time.

His plays are still being performed all around the world, even though he died some 400 years ago. Every one of us at some stage studied his plays at school. I've still got my notes if anybody wants them. On second thoughts, you might be better off taking your own notes.

William Shatner: a Canadian actor who is best known for his role as Captain Kirk on *Star Trek*.

Most recently he starred as attorney Denny Crane in *Boston Legal*. He is now regarded as one of the greatest comic actors.

wimp: someone who is soft and not prepared to put himself on the line.

One of the most offensive things you can call a bloke. When there was a crush as people rushed to get to this book on its release, there wouldn't have been any wimps there because they would've been too afraid they might get hurt.

Windies: West Indies cricket team.

They used to be a powerhouse and put fear into the Aussie batsmen. Not so much any more. Not that they need to. The Aussie batsmen somehow manage to put fear into themselves.

When you select your best **wingman**, make sure he's not a King Dick (page 111) or wanker (page 234). Chicks do not find these types attractive.

wingman: a bloke who helps his mate pick up.

His job is to chat to the best friend of the chick his mate is trying to pick up. A good wingman must be prepared to dance with that chick if necessary. Sometimes the wingman ends up

picking up and his mate doesn't. Against the run of play, his mate ended up unwittingly playing the wingman.

wonky: unsteady.
When you're sitting or standing on something that feels like it could give way any second. If I'm sitting on it, there's a fair chance it will.

work out: to exercise.
Often at the gym. A lot of blokes like telling people that they work out. Not as glamorous as it sounds when you see them at the gym coughing and spluttering and dripping in sweat.

wrote myself off: got really drunk.

X marks the spot. That's what it always says on a map that shows you where to find buried treasure. Well, it does in the movies. If you can't believe the movies, who can you believe. XXXX is a famous Queensland beer. We don't drink it in Melbourne because I reckon our beer here is so much better. XXX is a movie rating that got me excited just writing it, so probably better if I never see one. X is also used in the game noughts and crosses and is universally accepted as the way stupid people sign their name. Chicks put Xs at the bottom of a card to signify kisses. I always make sure I take them up on each one of those.

X marks the spot: the exact location of something.
You know when a player stamps on the ground to mark where he'll kick for goal? That's an 'X marks the spot' moment.

XL: extra large.
Clothing size. They do get bigger. There's also XXL and I think there's even an XXXL. I hope there's not an XXXXL. That would need a whole shop to itself.

> A word of warning.
> If you make a habit of ordering the **XL**-sized burger / fries / Kentucky fried etc, you'll end up wearing the XXXL size T-shirts and tracky-dacks.

Xmas: a lazy and easy way to write 'Christmas'.
Santa's flying around the world in a mad frenzy, delivering presents and we can't even be bothered writing the word 'Christmas' properly.

X-rated: adults only.
Material containing sexual content. A massive industry, so there must be a huge demand, and that doesn't include all the blokes who want to go and buy it but are too embarrassed to do so.

X-ray: something you have to show the extent of your injuries or illness.
I grew to hate X-rays – just when I thought I'd get a week off from playing because of a crook ankle / hip / knee, the X-ray would show nothing wrong. Sprung!

X-road: a lazy way of writing crossroad; the place where two roads cross each other.

Some people reach an X-road in their life but I've never had to worry about that. The Darl makes all my big decisions for me.

xylophone: a handy word in Scrabble when someone else put down 'phone'.

An old-fashioned musical instrument. Handy filler when you have to think of some X words that are not X-rated.

Gen Y (Generation Y) refers to the generation following mine (Generation X). It is also known as 'Generation Next'. Their birth dates range from the mid 1980s to the early 2000s. What sets them apart from my generation is their ability to use and understand technology like mobile phones, video games, iPods and computers. We do all right with those things but Gen Ys have mastered them and can use them with their eyes closed. Whenever I buy a new piece of technology, I throw it to my kids and say, 'Get it going and then show me the basics.'

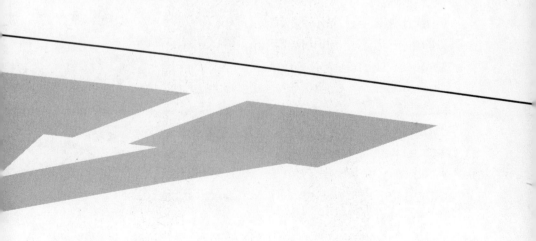

Y: text for 'why?'

When this comes from one of your kids, the answer is a simple 'Because I said so'. But that's too long to text. I might start a trend: BISS.

yabby: a fresh-water crustacean.

Not as big as a crayfish. They usually grow to around 20 centimetres. Yabbying is a great Australian pastime, which most kids have done at some stage. Yabbies are good eating too. My dad likes to cook them using his special secret recipe, which basically involves boiling them and adding salt. It's hard to keep an accurate record of yabby numbers because so many of them are in dams on farms. There's also no one who's willing to go around and count them.

yack: to talk about nothing in particular; a bit like 'chew the fat'.

Blokes are quite good at yacking about footy, the races and stuff like that, but only to other blokes.

yank: an American.

yank tank: an American car.

Refers to the really big outlandish ones. Some of the classic American cars look great and are imported by Australian car fanatics. If a car is considered a collector's item, then you can keep it as left-hand drive, which is great when you want to abuse them when they're passing you because the driver is right next to you. You can even poke him in the eye if you like.

yes man: someone who sucks up to the boss.
They just agree with everything the boss says, which must be hard if the boss ever sacks them: 'Yes, you're right. I'm hopeless at my job, a disgraceful employee and an embarrassment to my family. Thank you for sacking me. I am really honoured.'

yonks: a long time; ages.
I'd love just once to hear a judge sentence someone by putting them away for yonks.

YouTube: a video-sharing website that has become huge.
Anyone can upload a video and then everyone around the world can watch it. Pretty cool, hey? That's how Justin Bieber was discovered. Mmm, maybe not so cool.

yuk: the precursor to 'gross'; the main word used by kids about vegetables.

ZZZ is the international sound of sleeping and snoring. When someone is going to bed, they'll often say, 'I'm just going to get some zeds.' ZZ Top is a popular American band who have been around for years. They are known for their blues-based rock and long beards. In the off season they also pick up a bit of work playing Santa in some of the local department stores.

zebra: a black-and-white striped animal (of the four-legged kind).
I struggle with anything wearing black-and-white stripes. I know I'm not alone in that. Enough said.

zilch: nothing.
When you end up empty-handed after expecting something. What my dad would give me when I used to ask him for money.

zinger: a clever and funny line that puts someone in their place.
It's great when it happens but more often than not I think of something good to say after the person has left. I try to chase them and yell the line in their general direction but the moment is gone.

zit: pimple.
One of the worst things about being a teenager. Well, going through puberty's not much fun either. Not to mention having to do homework . . . and visiting Nanna.

zombie: an unmotivated person who is really boring to be around.
A lot of them go on to become parking inspectors.

zonked: tired.
Knackered. Totally exhausted. Needing a lie down. Just having written a big book.

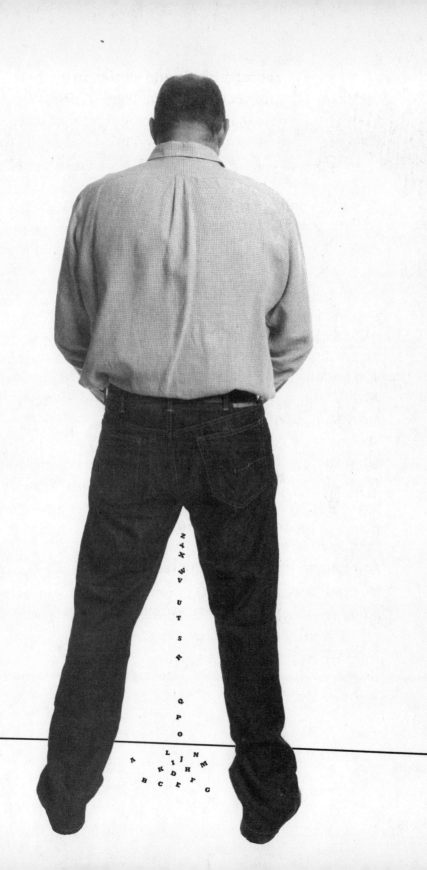

ACKNOWLEDGEMENTS

To Captain Cook – thanks for discovering Australia. Without you, I would've been up shit creek without a paddle. Good one, Cookie.

To Paul Calleja – thanks for helping me out with my home-work, mate. You're a dead-set legend.

To the great team behind the dictionary: my one-eyed pub-lisher, Andrea McNamara, and editor Bridget Maidment at Penguin and designer Nikki Townsend. Remember there's no 'I' in team, but there is in Billy!

To Nicky and the kids (Lucy, Ruby, Oscar and Max) – thanks for putting up with me and especially for your help with the chick words and teenage words throughout this book. And special thanks to Nicky for keeping everything on an even keel.

And last but not least, thanks to all you blokes out there for the great words and sayings I've heard over the drip trays in all those front bars. I tried to tell the Darl I was researching my book but she didn't believe me . . .